# Welcome!

## Celebrations with young children for the Church's year

## Jenny Pate

**McCrimmons**
Great Wakering, Essex, United Kingdom

This edition published in the United Kingdom in 2003 by
MCCRIMMON PUBLISHING CO. LTD.
10-12 High Street, Great Wakering, Essex  SS3 0EQ

Email: mccrimmons@dial.pipex.com
Website: www.mccrimmons.com


ISBN 0 85597 642 X

Cover design and layout: Nick Snode
Printed on 100gsn offset white
Body text set in 11.5pt Verdana, headings set in 32pt Mixage ITC medium italic
Printed and bound by Polestar Wheatons, Exeter

# Contents

# Foreword

One of the most successful developments of recent years has been the introduction in our parishes of what we call Children's Liturgy or Little Church. It is now quite normal, at the start of the principal Sunday Eucharist, to see happy youngsters heading off with one or two dedicated helpers to celebrate the first part of the Mass on their own. How did it all begin?

In 1973 a very helpful document was published in Rome. It was called Directory of Masses with Children. It had two central concerns: the first that we should take the Mass seriously; the second, that we should take children seriously. And so we read: 'Wherever the necessary facilities are available, it is appropriate to have a special Liturgy of the Word and homily for the children in a separate place not too far distant from the main body of the church. Then when the Eucharistic Liturgy begins they can be brought back to the place where, in the meantime, the adults have been celebrating their own Liturgy of the Word.'

That points to how it all began. But it also makes clear what it is we're doing. We are celebrating 'a special Liturgy of the Word and homily for the children'. What we are about is Liturgy – not minding the children, running a crèche or even a Sunday School.

And at this point, even the most willing can take fright: What does celebrating the Liturgy mean? How do we go about it? What help is available? Well, fear not! Welcome will provide most of what you need. First published in 1989 and now revised for re-publishing, Jenny Pate's work has stood the test of time and come to the rescue of many a harassed helper. Within a framework of worship, it ensures that Sunday by Sunday God's Word is heard and responded to in a way and at a level that is entirely appropriate for youngsters.

If you are a newly enlisted helper, this will give you confidence. If you are a more seasoned campaigner, you will find here a rich resource for your own initiatives.

+ Brian M Noble
Bishop of Shrewsbury

# *Celebrations with young children*

*Ezra the priest brought the Law before the assembly, consisting of men, women and children, old enough to understand... and Ezra read from the Law of God, translating and giving the sense, so that the people understood what was read."*

*Nehemiah 8:2-8*

*Sometimes, perhaps, if the necessary facilities are available, it will be appropriate to have a special Liturgy of the Word and Homily for the children in a separate place not too far distant from the main church (para 17).*

Directory on Children's Masses

## What guidelines are offered?

The following extract from the Directory on Children's Masses shows that the needs of children are to be considered seriously:

> *The Church has a duty to be specially concerned about the welfare of children who have been baptized but not yet fully initiated by the sacraments of Confirmation and the Eucharist, or who have only recently made their First Communion (para 1).*

Issued by the
Sacred Congregation of Divine Worship,
1st November 1973.

This book is primarily offered as a resource to parishes and schools. It is intended to enable them to initiate young children gradually into the 'mysteries of faith' which the community celebrates in the Eucharistic liturgy of each Sunday and some principal feasts. It seeks to do so in ways which are suited to the age and stage of development of young children. The celebrations outlined are centred round some of the main themes of the Liturgy of the Word of the particular Sunday or feast. This text is not intended to cover every aspect of the Liturgy of the Word or to be a lectionary for children's Masses. It is a practical resource for reflecting on and celebrating the Word of God with young children who are not yet capable of attending to or understanding the Word as proclaimed and celebrated with older children and adults.

## What does the celebration with young children offer?

- It introduces the children to important aspects of the Gospel message.
- It gives the children an opportunity to reflect on and celebrate the Word of God at their own level, at their own pace.
- It helps children to discover that the Word of God has meaning in their lives now, as children.
- It introduces children to some of the symbols and movements of the liturgy.
- It gives them the experience of being part of a community of faith and playing an active part in it.
- It gives the parish an opportunity to share its faith with its younger members. For many parishioners, of whatever age, who act as leaders, it is their opportunity to 'welcome with joy' the new young parishioners.
- It supports young families in their task of bringing up the children in the ways of faith.
- In a real way it helps develop the HOME-SCHOOL-PARISH Partnership.

## When does it take place?

This varies greatly from parish to parish and depends on the facilities available.

- In some parishes the children go directly to their celebration before Mass begins.
- In some parishes the whole congregation (children and adults) are welcomed by the celebrant at the start of Mass.
  The children are then invited by the leader or celebrant to withdraw to their own place. Often this is done ceremoniously by the celebrant handing the leader a children's Bible.
- In some parishes the children are with drawn after the opening prayer.
- In some parishes the children withdraw only for the homily.

Generally, the children return to the main congregation at the start of the Liturgy of the Eucharist (sometimes joining the offertory procession).

## Who is responsible for leading the celebration?

Recruiting leaders for this work is not such a difficult task. The skills needed are: sympathy for children, faith, a love of and familiarity with the Gospels and liturgy, and willingness to give time to share with others.

Consider inviting:

- young parents who are concerned about their children's faith and who want their children to find Mass meaningful and enjoyable.
- young people, teenagers who want to give some service to the church.
- people who enjoy working with children and perhaps have some experience in teaching, leading play groups, brownie/cub packs etc.
- retired parishioners whose children have grown up.
- anyone who sees the sense in this activity!

All involved say that they receive far more than they give and that the Word of God takes on a new and much deeper meaning for them as a result of their preparation for these celebrations with young children.

## Setting

Formal benches or chairs are not necessary. A bright, warm room with a piece of carpet for the children to sit on is all that's needed. If a school room is being used then it is very important that the furniture be re-arranged. The children should not sit at desks nor should the leader sit behind a teacher's desk. The setting should be appropriate for prayer and celebration rather than a religious education lesson. A special table/place should be set aside for the declaration of the gospel.

## Age Groups

Children from 3 – 10 years are attracted to this activity. To meet their needs it is important to separate them into older and younger age groups.

### Children aged seven and younger

The material in this book has been written with children of this age in mind.

Children younger than 6 and 7 years of age will enjoy the company of other children, the activities and singing. They will soon enter into the ritual and will probably join in some of the songs and prayers.

The 6 and 7 year olds will enter into the ritual and discussion (if given time to think and gather their thoughts) and understand the gospel message.

### Children older than seven

The prayer and songs suggested for the Introductory Rites may be appropriate with older children. Likewise the framework for the Liturgy of the Word would be suitable for any age group. However, children older than seven may be ready to hear fuller gospel texts and possibly additional readings such as the first reading of the day. This book should be used alongside other resources with older children.

All children will love lighting and blowing out the gospel candle.

# A suggested way of working

## Introductory Rites

In the Mass the introductory rites include Entrance Antiphon, Welcome, Penitential Rite, Gloria and Opening Prayer. This can be too heavy a demand on children's attention. Here the introductory rites take a more condensed form.

## Welcome

The Welcome is a time for:

- listening to what has happened during the week, at home e.g. How is your family? or at school e.g. Have you had school holidays yet?
- checking on birthdays and singing 'Happy Birthday'.
- welcoming newcomers.
- following up an activity from the previous week e.g. Are you still bored or did you pour out some of the happiness from the jugs? (3rd Sunday, Year C).

The Welcome will take more time in a 'Children's Liturgy of the Word' than in the parish Mass.

## Penitential Rite / Gloria / Opening Prayer

A Penitential Rite, Gloria and Opening Prayer are suggested. Whilst some groups might have time for all three, most will not, so only one of the three parts appears each Sunday. Preference might be given to one because of the liturgical season (e.g. Gloria during the Easter season). They are repeated regularly so that the children quickly remember them and join in.

## Liturgy of the Word

In the Mass the Liturgy of the Word includes a reading from the Old Testament, a responsorial Psalm, a second reading from the New Testament (generally a letter from St Paul), a Gospel Acclamation verse and the Gospel. This is followed by a Homily, the Creed and Bidding Prayers.

The Directory of Children's Masses (42) acknowledges that this can be too heavy a demand on children's attention. However, it states the Gospel should not be omitted. With young children this is all the more necessary. The adaptation offered here has been found to work well.

## Stop to think

Begin with the children's experience. God made them, continues to create them, and is at work in their daily lives through all their relationships and experiences.

Ask the children to stop and think about a particular aspect of their lives. It is important that they are given time (1-2 mins) to do this individually and in privacy. (Incidentally this might be the only opportunity for silence during the whole celebration).

## Share with one another

It is through recalling and telling our experiences that we begin to see their significance.

Invite the children to share their reflections. (The leader might draw out the significance with further questions.) Everyone who wishes to speak should be given the opportunity. Regular contributors might be persuaded to let others have 'first go' if they are assured of a hearing later.

In these first two steps we are preparing the children to hear the Gospel and receive its message in a practical way, by thinking about and reflecting on their own lives. Through this process the children will discover God who cares, loves and leads, who speaks to them and invites them to become friends/co-workers, bringing the Good News to their world.

## Gospel Acclamation

The Gospel is further prepared for

- by ceremoniously lighting the Gospel candle
- by singing the Gospel Acclamation

Invite a child to light the candle and encourage all the children to take a turn at this.

A number of Gospel acclamations are given on page 15, 29, 49, 104 and 106 appropriate for the liturgical seasons. Younger children love to repeat the same song over and over, but older ones (and leaders) might like a change. One variation would be to change the final words, picking up the Gospel message e.g. Alleluia, hear the Lord, let's not worry. (8th Sunday Year A) Another would be for children and leader to make up their own acclamations using tunes they know and like.

## Gospel

'Breaking the Word' is part of the experience of the People of God. We break and share the Word of the Gospel with young children in order to contribute to their living and understanding of the Christian way of life. We do so in ways that respect their age, development and experience.

However, in most of the Sunday Gospels there are too many ideas and concepts too deep for young children. One or two key phrases are enough to get the Gospel message across. In some cases where appropriate there is a fuller story form.

The Gospel can be read by the leaders or proclaimed by all the children. This second approach might be used when only one or two phrases of the Gospel are being proclaimed. These should be written on a large sheet of card and placed ceremoniously on the centre table/altar.

## Let's chat / Homily

It would be all too easy to preach at the children at this point. A better approach (and a style that Jesus used) would be to allow the children to make a free response. With some prompting they willingly give their reaction to the Gospel, saying what it means to them; what difference, if any, it makes to their lives.

## Creed / Bidding Prayers

You may not have time to include these elements of the Liturgy of the Word.

The time available for celebrating with children varies from Mass to Mass, from venue to venue. However, you should aim to include a creed and bidding prayers with children over the age of seven. Most younger children at this point of the celebration have had enough words: activities are called for. The most usual is some kind of drawing or colouring. The children make as prayerful, and as much a community response in this way as they might with more words. Drawing and colouring are ways in which children can interiorise, remember and express the Gospel message for themselves and others. Nevertheless, from time to time prayers are included in the material and the children might be invited to say a bidding prayer before returning to the church.

- Most groups find it is best to end on an 'elastic' type of activity. The amount of time available depends on the priest and people celebrating the Mass. Sometimes the call to return to the main congregation comes quite suddenly; other times the wait might seem like an eternity. (See Closing Activities p. 11)

## For your convenience

*In the majority of cases the complete text needed for each celebration is printed on one page.*

*The songs and prayers for each season are given on the introductory page for each season.*

*The Gospel acclamations are given on pages 15, 29, 49, 104 and 106.*

*In addition all the commonly used texts of prayers, songs and acclamations are printed on the end papers at the front and back of the book.*

# Adapting this material for other settings

This material is intended for parish use though with some adaptation it might be used in other settings.

**At home by:**

- parents and children as preparation for Sunday Mass.
- parents and children as a way of deepening and sharing their faith together.
- grandparents who take responsibility for the formation of their grandchildren.
- godparents who wish to help parents in their task of bringing their children up in the Christian faith.
- adults who enjoy the company of children and who find sharing faith with them a stimulating and refreshing experience.

**At school by teachers:**

- preparing class and school assemblies.
- looking ahead to the Sunday liturgy.
- helping young children to know more about Jesus.

# Planning and evaluation

A successful liturgy or catechetical experience does not just happen. It needs careful thought and time spent in preparation. Here are some of the ways in which leaders and parish groups prepare:

- weekly meetings to read and reflect upon the Sunday readings.
- monthly meetings to talk over the difficulties and successes, to check continuity, share ideas and plan ahead. (See evaluation checklist). Depending on the number of leaders, rotas and responsibilities are arranged in advance. (See planning checklist page 9).
- half-yearly meetings with other parish groups to exchange ideas and experiences. A speaker is often invited to these meetings to help widen and deepen the leaders' experience and understanding of celebrating liturgy with young children. Often a leader from another parish is the greatest help!
- art and music workshops for the children before special seasons, e.g. Advent, Christmas, Lent, Easter, Whitsun. Just about everyone in the parish can be invited to help in these workshops.

Misunderstandings about this activity may arise in the parish. Some parishioners see it as 'child-minding' or a 'holy playgroup' with little or no connection with the Sunday liturgy. The leaders' response is often to overburden themselves with elaborate displays of art work to prove the content of this activity. Far better to invite anxious parents and parishioners to some of the planning meetings so that they can have a better idea of what happens.

---

## Sample evaluation checklist

### CELEBRATION

What went well, what did the children most enjoy?............................................................

.........................................................................

What were the difficulties?...............................

.........................................................................

Is there a reasonable level of continuity?...........

.........................................................................

What changes need to be made? .....................

.........................................................................

### RELATIONSHIPS

Is there sufficient liaison, partnership with the celebrant?......................................................

.........................................................................

Who else do we need to liaise with? .................

.........................................................................

How are the relationships between our Little Church' and other groups or individuals in the parish? ......................................................

.........................................................................

Is there anyone we need to say 'thanks' to? ......

.........................................................................

### THINKING AHEAD

What long-term planning do we need to give thought to?......................................................

.........................................................................

**N.B. Don't take understanding and communication for granted.**

# Sample planning checklist

| MONTHLY OVERVIEW | Leader | Assisted by |
|---|---|---|
| Sunday, 1st July | ................................... | ................................... |
| Sunday, 8th July | ................................... | ................................... |
| Sunday, 15th July | ................................... | ................................... |
| Sunday, 22nd July | ................................... | ................................... |
| Sunday, 29th July | ................................... | ................................... |

## WEEKLY CHECKLIST

Who will be responsible for preparing the room, i.e. holy table, heating, chairs, crayons etc.? ...................................

Who will be responsible for liaising with the celebrant? ...................................

Who will take the book and lead the procession out of church? ...................................

Welcome and Introductory Rites led by ...................................

Stop to Think and Share with one another led by ...................................

(If there's more than one age group) led by ...................................

...................................

...................................

When the children reassemble as one big group

Gospel candle lit by ...................................

Gospel introduced by ...................................

Gospel proclaimed by ...................................

Homily (Let's chat) led by ...................................

If there's more than one age group then led by ...................................

(return to earlier groupings) ...................................

...................................

...................................

## ACTIVITY

What activity follows? ...................................

...................................

What can the children take home? ...................................

...................................

Who will be the timekeeper? ...................................

Who will be the musician? ...................................

Who will tidy up after the Mass! ...................................

# Closing activities – bridge to the Eucharistic liturgy

The children's celebrations need to end in an 'elastic type' activity. It is difficult to predict how much time might be left. All sorts of circumstances bring the altar servers too soon, or late, to recall the children into church for the Eucharistic liturgy. It is not surprising that leaders tend to use the time in colouring a picture that can be finished later at home. Whilst it can be a useful activity and a further stimulus for the family to reflect on the day's readings, it may become a burden that neither leader nor children can carry. The celebration might end in other ways, for example:

## Songs

Singing can be quite the best activity and can prepare the children for the eucharistic rite (see page 230). Such songs will help them to participate in the continuing celebration of the Mass and unite them with the rest of the congregation. (Avoid a hymn practise; see art and music workshop in the planning section on page 10.)

## Prayer

- Silent prayer. Children left free to make their own response.
- Prayers of praise and thanks. Each child in turn could say thank you to God for some new thought or awareness that has occurred to them, or for something that happened to them during the week. All could reply to each prayer with a phrase such as 'Lord God, you are wonderful'.
- Prayers of petition. Expressed in a similar manner.

## Mime

In small groups (so that everyone has a part) the children could mime the Gospel and continue with what they think happened next.

Have ready simple props and costumes that can be quickly removed.

## Thoughts for the week

What has been learnt might be easily summed-up with a thought for the week. This one sentence might be taken home or put on the parish notice board. The children might need it written-up so that they can copy. Be careful about presuming writing skills.

Try to avoid phrases such as 'be kind'; encourage the children to be specific, aiming for something achievable. Follow up responses such as 'be kind' with 'yes, but who will you be kind to and when and how... ?' Give your own thoughts too.

This way of showing what has gone on in the celebration might be more useful than an unfinished picture which is hard to decipher.

## One-minute art

- Cut out cardboard figures that can have paper clothes added to help the children focus on the gospel, e.g. poor man, rich man. Hang paper sandwich boards onto the figures, or give them speech balloons.
- Felt pictures: shapes that can be arranged and rearranged on sandpaper.
- Plasticine clay models.
- Collages or models (perhaps using Lego) built up week-by-week. The children might like to make something at home and then add their contribution on Sunday.

Focus on the season rather than just the day. Suggestions for activities are given at the beginning of each liturgical season.

As well as bringing to a close the children's own celebration, these activities are a bridge to the Eucharistic liturgy.
The children can be helped to understand that with Jesus, they can offer to God all that they have done and learned.

> **Remember:**
>
> **All the material on the following pages needs the imagination and creativity of children and leaders to bring it alive. God speaks through our imagination, let him have plenty of say!**

# Advent

## The four Sundays before Christmas

Advent begins the Church's Year. It is a time of preparation for the Second Coming (though we are always preparing for Christ's return). The word Advent means Coming. The readings in the first week of Advent set our thoughts in this context. The season recalls how the people of God longed for the Saviour, and concludes with the celebrations of Christmas: the Incarnation, God becoming a person just like us!

These ideas can't be easily explained to children. It's enough for them to feel a sense of longing (not difficult for children at this time of year) and to be happy to celebrate God becoming a person just like me.

## ADVENT ACTIVITIES (1)

Some of the following activities may help to create a sense of longing and rejoicing.

### Advent wreath

- A circle of evergreen leaves
  *representing God's everlasting love.*

- Four candles
  *representing Jesus light of the world one for each week of Advent.*

- One candle is pink
  *representing God's free gift of forgiveness.*

- The other three candles are purple
  *representing our desire for forgiveness.*

- One white candle is placed in the centre on Christmas Day
  *representing Jesus, the Light of the World.*

Much of the symbolism will puzzle or confuse the children and if explained, might be best explained week by week. They will enjoy the weekly countdown.

## ADVENT ACTIVITIES (2)

### *Jesse Tree*

This is simply Jesus' family tree. It begins as an undecorated tree and week by week pictures or symbols representing Jesus' ancestors and relations are added to the tree. On Christmas Day a star is placed at the top, other decorations are added too: a paper star crib can be easily made by the children.

The children might like to make their own family tree as Jesus is part of their family too.

### *Crib*

During Advent prepare a frieze of Bethlehem by night with busy streets, inns and people. Prepare all the crib figures, but place only the ox and the ass in the stable. On Christmas Day as the Gospel story is told the children can add the other figures.

## INTRODUCTORY RITE

## Sign of the Cross

**Song** – God sends his Son

Mary Oswin

© Mary Oswin

The world was in darkness
And nobody knew
The way to the Father
As you and I do
They needed a light
That would show them the way;
And the great light shone
On Christmas Day.

## Say or sing – Lord, have mercy

Seoirse Bodley

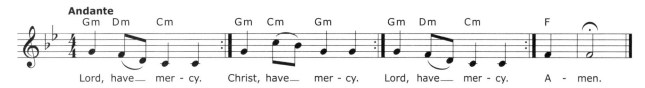

Lord have Mercy

**R. Lord have mercy.**

Christ have mercy

**R. Christ have mercy.**

Lord have mercy

**R. Lord have mercy.**

© Seoirse Bodley

## Opening Prayer

*Let us pray*

| | |
|---|---|
| Father, | help us to want |
| As we light our | true happiness |
| Advent candles | that lasts for ever and ever, |
| | Amen. |

*End of Introductory Rite, turn to Sunday text* ➤

## Gospel Acclamation – Like a sea without a shore

Estelle White

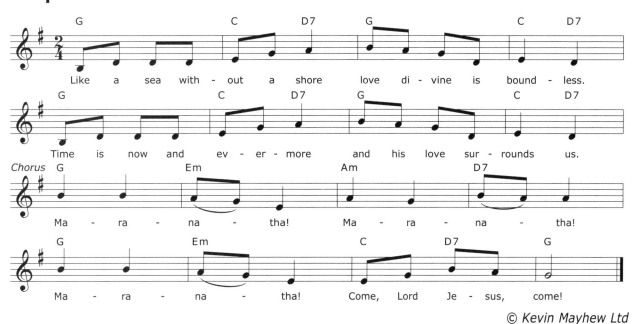

© Kevin Mayhew Ltd

*or say:*

**Come Lord Jesus, come**

or (Come, Lord Jesus, Marantha!)

**ADVENT**

| | |
|---|---|
| **Year A** | begins on page 16 |
| **Year B** | begins on page 20 |
| **Year C** | begins on page 24 |

# Don't forget

## Welcome

## Let's sing and say *(If celebrating the Introductory Rite, turn to page 14)*

*Quietly by yourselves*

## Stop to think

Are people very busy at the moment getting things ready?
What are they getting ready for? What sort of things are they doing?

*When each child has had time to think*

## Share with one another

Are you busy too? What are you busy doing?
Will you forget to get ready? What will you forget?
Jesus wants us to be ready to celebrate his birthday.

## Gather around the Advent wreath

*and light one purple candle*
Jesus also wants us to be ready for when he comes
again (not as a baby); we mustn't forget that he will.

*Welcome the Gospel with a song. (Gospel acclamations page 15)*
*All stand        (adapted from Matthew 24:42)*

### Gospel

Jesus said,
"Don't forget, be ready,
because one day I will return
and no one knows when."

This is the Gospel of the Lord.

**Praise be to you Lord Jesus Christ.**

*All sit*

## Let's chat *(some suggestions)*

Don't forget to be ready for Jesus when he comes again. How can we be ready?
At this time of year everyone is promising to be good and everyone is cheerful.
This is exactly how to get ready for Jesus.
When Jesus does come again he will be so pleased and happy to see you.
This week let's get ready for Jesus' birthday by getting into the Christmas mood?
What does that mean? – happy, hopeful, encouraging, cheerful. (Help the children to think of
practical examples.)

# Get ready

## Welcome

## Let's sing and say  (If celebrating the Introductory Rite, turn to page 14)

*Quietly by yourselves*
## Stop to think

Have you been doing any shopping?
Have you noticed that there are lots of people collecting money? Who are they collecting for?

*When each child has had time to think*
## Share with one another

Why do you think they bother to collect money?
It can be great fun watching the collectors, sometimes they dress up.
Have you seen any of them dressed as Father Christmas?
Sometimes they annoy us, they get in our way and pester us for money which we don't want to give away. They can get on our nerves. If they didn't bother to collect money, what would happen to the people they are collecting for?

## Gather around the Advent Wreath

*and light two purple candles*

This week we hear from John the Baptist (who looked odd and used to get on some people's nerves). He is Jesus' cousin.

*Welcome the Gospel with a song. (Gospel acclamations page 15)*
*All stand        (adapted from Matthew 3:7-12)*

> ## Gospel
>
>  John said,
> "Don't pretend to be good.
> Some people think they are good just because they go to Church.
> You must do more, you must help others, don't pass by those who need you."

This is the Gospel of the Lord. **Praise be to you Lord Jesus Christ.**

*All sit*
## Let's chat  *(some suggestions)*

Who needs your help this week? Could you give to the poor?
Could you help at your Christmas Fair?
What could you do to make someone happy?

# Be happy –
# Jesus brings good times

## Welcome

## Let's sing and say (If celebrating the Introductory Rite, turn to page 14)

*Quietly by yourselves*

## Stop to think

Have you put your Christmas decorations up?
Which is your favourite?
What do you like about Christmas decorations?

*When each child has had time to think*

## Share with on another

Chat about Christmas decorations.

Christmas decorations get us into the Christmas
mood. We love them. They sometimes make us feel that Christmas is already here.
How will we know when Christmas is really here? (All sorts of good things happen.)
Are you beginning to wonder how much longer you'll have to wait? Do you keep asking mum?

## Gather around the Advent wreath

*And light two purple candles*

John sent his friends to see Jesus.
He wondered if Jesus was the great king they all hoped for or if they would have to wait
much longer.

*Welcome the Gospel with a song. (Gospel acclamations page 15)*

*All stand* (adapted from Matthew 11:4-11)

### Gospel

 Jesus said to John's friends,
"Go back and tell John that
all sorts of good things are happening
and he will know that the time has
come."

Then Jesus said about John,

"John has been a great sign.
He was sent to get you ready
for my coming."

*All sit*

### Let's chat (some suggestions)

Are you keeping up your Christmas mood
ready for Jesus' coming?
Perhaps if we don't pester mum, if we
remember to say thanks, if we don't fight, we
too might be a sign to everyone that there
are good times ahead.

This is the Gospel of the Lord.
**Praise be to you Lord Jesus Christ.**

# Mary's baby is God's Son

*Welcome*

*Let's sing and say* *(If celebrating the Introductory Rite, turn to page 14)*

*Quietly by yourselves*

*Stop to think*

Are you beginning to wonder about Christmas?
Are you wondering whether everything will turn out right?

*When each child has had time to think*

*Share with one another*

What are you wondering about?
What do you think the other people in your family are wondering about? Perhaps they're wondering if Christmas will be alright, and if everyone will be safe and happy?

*Gather around the Advent wreath*

*and light all four purple candles*

Joseph heard the news about Mary's baby and he began to wonder if everything would be all right.

*Welcome the Gospel with a song (Gospel acclamations page 15)*

*All stand* *(adapted from Matthew 1:18-25)*

### Gospel

When Joseph heard the news about Mary, he began to wonder if everything was going to be all right.

One night he had a dream.
In the dream an angel said to him,

"Don't worry Joseph,
Mary's baby is God's Son."

Joseph woke up and knew that everything was all right.
He trusted God.

He and Mary lived very happily together.

This is the Gospel of the Lord.

**Praise be to you Lord Jesus Christ.**

*All sit*

### Let's chat *(some suggestions)*

What do mums and dads wonder about?

What can you do to help Christmas be a good time for everyone?

How can you help everyone to live happily together in your house?

Jesus,
please make our homes happy places
this Christmas,
keep everyone safe,
and take away mum's and dad's worries.

We know you can do this
because you are God's Son.

# Waiting

## Welcome

## Let's sing and say (If celebrating the Introductory Rite, turn to page 14)

*Quietly by yourselves*

## Stop to think

What do you hate waiting for: your tea, school to finish? Perhaps you hate waiting for mum to finish talking, the news to finish on TV or your favourite TV programme to start. Maybe it's waiting for a friend to call or for them to be ready to play. Perhaps it's just waiting for other people.

*When each child has had time to think*

## Share with one another

What do you hate waiting for? Sometimes when visitors are expected we get ourselves and the house ready. If they don't arrive when we expect them, we get bored and we begin to think about and do other things. We almost forget that they are coming. If they are a long time we begin to think they have forgotten us. Then suddenly the door bell goes, they're here and all the fun begins.

## Gather around the Advent wreath

*and light one purple candle*

Jesus said before he went back to his Father, that he would come again. He might come anytime and we must be ready.

*Welcome the Gospel with a song (Gospel acclamations page 15)*

*All stand         (adapted from Mark 13:33-37)*

---

### Gospel

Jesus said to his friends,
"Be ready
because you never know
when the time
for me to return will come."

---

This is the Gospel of the Lord.
**Praise be to you Lord Jesus Christ.**

*All sit (don't scare the children with stories of sudden appearances, judgements etc.)*

## Let's chat (some suggestions)

When would you like Jesus to come back?
What do you think he will look like?
He will be so glad to see you because you are his friend. (He will be glad to see me too.) What will you say to each other?
Are you expecting any friends to visit you this Christmas?
What will you have ready for them?
What should we get ready for when Jesus comes?

# Get ready

*Welcome*

*Let's sing and say*  (If celebrating the Introductory Rite, turn to page 14)

*Quietly by yourselves*

## Stop to think

Have you been buying anything new for Christmas?
Have you been buying new clothes?

*When each child has had time to think*

## Share with one another

*(Let the children describe the clothes they've
bought or hope to get.)*

We all love to have new things for Christmas.
We like to look our best. Sometimes we can't afford all new things.
It's too expensive, so we have to choose carefully and see what we can manage.

## Gather around the Advent wreath

*and light two purple candles*

Jesus' cousin, John the Baptist, is telling us
to get ready, to be at our best for Jesus.

*Welcome the Gospel with a song
(Gospel acclamations page 15)
All stand      (adapted from Mark 1:3-5)*

 **Gospel**

John said:
"Prepare a way for Jesus,
get yourselves straight,
say sorry for your sins."

This is the Gospel of the Lord.

**Praise be to you Lord Jesus Christ.**

*All sit*

## Let's chat  *(some suggestions)*

What does he mean 'get yourselves straight?'
To sort ourselves out, to change all our ways
so that we'll be at our best is impossible.

Let's choose one thing that we can put right
so that there will be something new about us
on Christmas Day. Make a list and choose

- Go to bed when I am told
- Get my own things ready for school
- Don't push in the line at school...

*(Let the children add their own)*

# Joy

*Welcome*

*Let's sing and say*  (If celebrating the Introductory Rite, turn to page 14)

*Quietly by yourselves*

## Stop to think

Are you having a school party?
Do you know anyone who's planning a night out?
Are mum and dad celebrating with friends?

*When each child has had time to think*

## Share with one another

What is the favourite dance at parties?
Can anyone show us? Everyone is very happy at the moment, there is plenty of rejoicing and celebrating. Anyone would think Christmas was here already.
We are having a good time but there are better times ahead.
Don't get too excited.

## Gather around the Advent wreath

*and light two purple candles and the pink one*
John the Baptist is telling us not to get too excited.
There are better times ahead, times that will bring real happiness.

*Welcome the Gospel with a song.  (Gospel acclamations page 15)*
*All stand*      *(adapted from John 1:6-8, 27-28)*

### Gospel

Everyone thought John was going to be the Great King, and they all began to get excited.
But John said:
"I am not the Great King that God has promised to send, someone else is coming after me, and he is much more important than I am. In fact, he is so great that I am not even good enough to untie his shoe-laces.!"

A. J. McCallen

This is the Gospel of the Lord.

**Praise be to you Lord Jesus Christ.**

*All sit*

### Let's chat  (some suggestions)

It's good to have parties and be happy, but we would be fools if we thought this was complete happiness.
The happiness at a party can be spoilt if someone calls you a name or upsets you, and it is soon over anyway; parties don't last forever. We can enjoy our parties but let's think about what will really make us happy, long-lasting happiness.
What will make us happy?
John is really telling us not to be fooled.
Think of one thing you can do for someone you know to make them really happy.

# God keeps his promise

**Welcome**

**Let's sing and say**  (If celebrating the Introductory Rite, turn to page 14)

*Quietly by yourselves*
**Stop to think**

Have you received any Christmas cards? Did anyone surprise you with a card?
Have you forgotten to send anyone a card?

*When each child has had time to think*
**Share with one another**

Listen to stories about giving, receiving Christmas cards. We love to be given cards as
it shows that people have remembered us. We like to be remembered at Christmas.
It makes us sad if we are forgotten.

**Gather around the Advent wreath**

*and light all four candles*
Today we hear that God has not forgotten us.
He promised to send us his Son and today
we hear that promise coming true.

*Welcome the Gospel with a song.*
*(Gospel acclamations page 15)*
*All stand  (adapted from Luke 1:26-38)*

---

**Gospel**

One day
God sent his Messenger
to a town called Nazareth
to a girl called Mary
who was engaged
to a man called Joseph.

The Messenger said:
  "Rejoice, Mary
  for the Lord has blessed you,
  and he is with you now!"

Mary didn't know what to say
and she wondered what this meant.
But the Messenger said:
  "Do not be afraid –
  God is very pleased with you."
  "Listen!
  You are going to have a baby
  and you will call him Jesus."

Then Mary said:
  "I am the servant of God.
  I am glad to do whatever he wants!"

A. J. McCallen

---

This is the Gospel of the Lord.  **Praise be to you Lord Jesus Christ.**

*All sit*  **Let's chat**  *(some suggestions)*

Jesus is going to come and live in the world. The Christmas dream is going to come true.
God has not forgotten us. In all the excitement have you forgotten anyone?
Should you be saying thanks to anyone?
Try and keep your promise to be good this week.

# Jesus will come again

## Welcome

## Let's sing and say
*(If celebrating the Introductory Rite, turn to page 14)*

*Quietly by yourselves*
## Stop to think
The candle light looks lovely. Do you like looking at lights?
Who is the first family to have a Christmas tree up in your road?
What are the lights like? Where are the best Christmas lights in your area?

*When each child has had time to think*
## Share with one another

*Share stories about favourite Christmas lights. Point out that at this time of year it gets dark early so it's a good time to have lights because we can notice them.*
Have you noticed the moon and stars?
It has to be a clear night and you need to turn off the room light.
Do you know that the stars have names? Does anyone know them?
Have you noticed that we don't always see every bit of the moon?

## Gather around the Advent wreath

*and light one purple candle*
Let's enjoy the light of our purple candle. How it cheers the room up.
It's a sign of all the good things to come.

*Welcome the Gospel with a song. (Gospel acclamations – page 15)*
*All stand      (adapted from Luke 21:25-28, 34-36)*

### Gospel

Jesus said,
   "There will be signs in the sun and moon and stars.
These signs will tell you that I am coming back.
Be happy to see them.
Don't forget me.
Be ready."

This is the Gospel of the Lord.

**Praise be to you Lord Jesus Christ.**

*All sit*
## Let's chat *(some suggestions)*
What do you think the signs will be?
When would you like Jesus to come back?

What do you think will happen when Jesus returns?

Do you think people have forgotten him?
Perhaps you could draw the signs.
Would you like to say Twinkle, Twinkle Little Star before you go back into the church?

# Get ready

## Welcome

## Let's sing and say *(If celebrating the Introductory Rite, turn to page 14)*

*Quietly by yourselves*

## Stop to think

What's happening in your house? Is anyone buying cards or presents?
Who is going to sort out the decorations? Who is going to put the tree up?
Who is going to do the extra shopping?
Who is going to clean up so that the house is at its best?

*When each child has had time to think*

## Share with one another

When the children have finished sharing their answers draw their discussion further.

Is it all mum's job? She must get tired. Who else can help? How can you help?
At this time of year mum (and teachers in school) often say, "Listen to me. If you don't calm down you will never be ready and we won't bother with Christmas celebrations."

Sometimes we wonder whether Christmas is worth the bother.

## Gather around the Advent wreath

*and light two purple candles*

Today John the Baptist, Jesus' cousin, is telling us to get ready for Jesus and he is telling us how to get ready. We must listen to him.

*Welcome the Gospel with a song. (Gospel acclamations – page 15)*

*All stand      (adapted from Luke 3:4-6)*

### Gospel

John said,
   "**Prepare for Jesus** by doing things his way.

So don't be miserable because you can't have everything you want, don't be a show off bragging about what you are doing or getting,
don't wriggle out of jobs, and don't torment other people."

This is the Gospel of the Lord.

**Praise be to you Lord Jesus Christ.**

*All sit*

### Let's chat *(some suggestions)*

Is it worth the bother getting ready for Christmas, buying cards and presents, making decorations? Why?
Is it worth the bother doing as John says (recall each step)?
Why, what difference will it make?

Make a list (draw or write) of all your preparations.

### LOOK AHEAD

**Leaders: Next week, you will need materials for colouring and drawings of an Advent Wreath or paper to draw on.**

# Joy to everyone

## Welcome

### Let's sing and say *(If celebrating the Introductory Rite, turn to page 14)*

*Quietly by yourselves*

### Stop to think

Have you spent all your pocket money on presents and cards? Are you 'broke'?
Are you glad that you have spent all your money on presents? Why?

*When each child has had time to think*

### Share with one another

Well done for being so generous!
Your presents will bring others happiness and you will enjoy their happiness too!
Did you notice people collecting money at the shops? Who were they collecting for?

### Gather around the Advent wreath

*and light two purple candles and one pink one*

Look at the pink candle: it is a sign of happiness.
Think of all the great happiness you are going to give people with your presents.

*Welcome the Gospel with a song. (Gospel acclamations – page 15)*
*All stand        (adapted from Luke 3:10-15)*

### Gospel

Lots of people asked John,
"What's the right thing to do?"
John said,
  "Share what you have with each other,
  if you have two of something
  give one away.
  If you have plenty of food to eat
  share with people who are short of food."

This is the Gospel of the Lord.

**Praise be to you Lord Jesus Christ.**

*All sit*

### Let's chat *(some suggestions)*

At the moment we are trying to do what John says especially when we give to collections.

Is anyone having a school Christmas party?
How can you share your food?
Who could you share you food with?
Do you think it's a good idea?

*(Leaders put the children into sharing groups with one felt tip pen per group.*
*Each child needs a picture of an Advent Wreath to colour or paper to draw on.)*

Think about all the happiness around at this time of year. Don't forget to share your pink felt tip or crayon and if you have to wait or do without think of people who have to do without so many things at Christmas.

# The promise will come true

## Welcome

## Let's sing and say *(If celebrating the Introductory Rite, turn to page 14)*

*Quietly by yourselves*

## Stop to think

Do people keep saying "if you promise to be good...
Have you promised to be good? Who have you promised?

*When each child has had time to think*

## Share with one another

Is it easy to keep such a promise? Is it easy to keep a promise to send a card or buy a present? Is it easy to keep a promise to be kind to everyone all the time?

## Gather around the Advent wreath

*and light all four candles*

Mary was a young and poor girl but she was so glad that God gave her a chance to be helpful.

*Welcome the Gospel with a song. (Gospel acclamations – page 15)*

*All stand        (adapted from Luke 1:39-44)*

### Gospel

One day, Mary heard that her cousin, Elizabeth, was going to have a baby.
So she went as quickly as she could into the hills to the town where Elizabeth lived.

Mary went into Elizabeth's house and said "Hello, how are you?"
And Elizabeth replied,
"I am proud that you have come to visit me because the Lord has given you a special blessing!
He has given you a special child!"
Then Mary said
"I praise the Lord for he is good

He makes me glad!
I am young and I am poor,
and yet he comes and chooses me!
And from now on,
everyone will say that he has blessed me".

"The Lord is strong, the Lord is generous stretching out his hand to help the sick, feeding hungry people with good food, looking after people everywhere!

"Long ago he said that he would help us.
Now the Lord has kept his promise perfectly.
He has not forgotten his own people
He has come to rescue them
and keep them safe."

A. J. McCallen

This is the Gospel of the Lord. **Praise be to you Lord Jesus Christ.**

*All sit* ## Let's chat

*(some suggestions)*

God keeps his promises perfectly.
He promised to send his Son and he did.
We should thank him.

We can't keep our promises perfectly but we can be like Mary always taking every chance we can to be helpful.
Ask Mary to help you to take the chances you are given to be helpful.

# Christmas

## Up to and including Baptism of the Lord

The praise of the angels who sang 'Glory to God in the highest heavens and peace on earth' is the key note of the season.

The source of this joy is the Incarnation. God becoming a person just like me!

### INTRODUCTORY RITE

### Sign of the Cross

### Penitential Rite

May almighty God
have mercy on us
forgive us
and take away all our sadness.
Amen.

### Song – Glory be to God on high

Traditional

To the tune of Angels we have heard on high

Mighty Lord and heav'nly King,
Jesus Christ the only Son.
Mighty Lord and Lamb of God,
Praise we all and sing as one.

*Gloria in excelsis Deo.*

Jesus, bearer of our sins,
Show us mercy, hear our prayer.
You who sit at God's right hand,
Show us mercy, hear our prayer.

You alone, the Holy One,
Jesus Christ and mighty Lord.
With the Spirit you are one,
With the Father in accord.

## Opening Prayer

*Let us pray*

Father,

May we your children
Who celebrate the birth of Jesus

Learn to see the good things promised
and given to us by you.
We ask this as friends of Jesus.

Amen.

*End of Introductory Rite, turn to Sunday text* ➤

## Gospel Acclamation – Eight-fold Alleluia

Traditional

Al - le - lu - ia, al - le - lu - ia, al - le - lu - ia, al - le - lu - ia,

al - le - lu - ia, al - le - lu - ia, al - le - lu - ia, al - le - lu - ia.

**CHRISTMAS**

**Year A** begins on page 32

**Year B** begins on page 34

**Year C** begins on page 37

# God becomes a baby

## Welcome

Let's pray the angels' prayer

**Glory to God in the highest
and peace to his people on earth.**

(If celebrating the Introductory Rite, turn to page 28)

*Quietly by yourself*
## Stop to think

Are you wearing your best clothes?
Is everything at home looking its best?

Is everyone at home trying hard to be kind and patient?

*When each child has had time to think*
## Share with one another

Share stories. Admire clothes.

Everyone is at their best today to give glory to God.
Everyone is smiling to give a happy feeling and peace to each other.

## Gather around the Advent candle

*Light all four candles then towards the end of the song place the white candle in the centre.*

*Welcome the Gospel with a song*
*(Music setting can be found on page 14)*

> The world was in darkness
> And nobody knew.
> The way to the Father
> As you and I do.
> They needed a light
> That would show them the way.
> And the great light shone
> on Christmas Day.
>
> Mary Oswin

*All stand (could be mimed by the children) (adapted from Luke 2:7-20)*

## Gospel

Jesus was born in Bethlehem – in a stable
because there was no room for him at the Inn.

This happened at night time,
and as usual the shepherds were out in the fields
looking after their sheep.

But suddenly the sky was filled with light
and they saw the Messenger of God!
At first they were afraid.
But then the Messenger said:

"Do not be afraid.
I have some good news for you
and for everyone else as well.

'Jesus, the Lord, has been born this very night.
You will find him wrapped in baby clothes
and lying in a stable in Bethlehem."

Then the shepherds could hear the sound of many people singing:

"Glory to God in the highest
and peace to his people on earth."

The shepherds didn't waste a minute.
They quickly found the stable,
they found Mary and Joseph and the baby,
and they told them everything they had heard.
Mary listened carefully to this story
and she kept all these things in her mind.

Then the shepherds went back to their sheep
thanking God for everything they had seen and heard.

A. J. McCallen

This is the Gospel of the Lord.
**Praise be to you Lord Jesus Christ.**

## Let's sing

Which carols do you know?
Sing as many as you can to give God glory before going back into Church.
Remember to smile at everyone today to give peace to God's people on earth.

# Holy Family

## Welcome

## Let's praise God! *(If celebrating the Introductory Rite, turn to page 28)*

*Quietly by yourselves*

## Stop to think

Where are you not allowed to play because it's 'dangerous'?
What are you not allowed to do because it's 'dangerous'?
What are you not allowed to do on your own?

*When each child has had time to think*

## Share with one another

*Let the children tell about their restrictions.*

Why do you think mum/dad make these rules? Mum and dad are always praying that God will keep you safe and he does. Have you ever heard them say 'Thank God you're safe'? or 'Thank God she's all right'?

## Light the Gospel candle

*by the crib if you have one*

This week we hear that Jesus was in
danger and Mary and Joseph had to leave suddenly to keep him safe.

*Welcome the Gospel. Sing Alleluia. (See page 29)*
*All stand (adapted from Matthew 2:13-15, 19-23)*

### Gospel

Jesus, Mary and Joseph had a visit from three wise men. After the wise men had left, an angel spoke to Joseph in a dream.

"Get up Joseph,
take Jesus and Mary and escape into Egypt.

There is danger, Herod doesn't want anyone else to be King.
He intends to do Jesus great harm."

Joseph got up.
He took Mary and Jesus into Egypt where they lived safely for a while.

When the danger was over they went to live in Nazareth.

A. J. McCallen

This is the Gospel of the Lord.
**Praise be to you Lord Jesus Christ.**

*All sit*

## Let's chat *(some suggestions)*

Are you glad Jesus escaped?
When we are in danger who can help?
Others? (Encourage the children to name adults they can trust)

Let's pray together:

Lord Jesus, help us to listen
when we are warned about dangers.

Lord hear us, **Lord please hear us**.

Lord Jesus, take care of all children
who have no mum and dad to take care of them. Lord hear us...

# God's plan

## Welcome

We are still celebrating Christmas, one of the happiest times of year.

## Let's praise God  (If celebrating the Introductory Rite, turn to page 28)

*Quietly by yourselves*

### Stop to think

Think back over Christmas and all the good
times that happened.
Which was your favourite moment?
Whose idea was it? Who planned it?

*When each child has had time to think*

### Share with one another

Did you make any plans for Christmas
(presents, surprises, visits etc)?
Did they work out? Did they bring lots of happiness?
Share stories of successful and unsuccessful plans.

## Light the Gospel candle  By the crib if you have one

This week we think back over Christmas and see how it was all God's plan. God's plan for
Jesus to be born. It really did work out well.

*Welcome the Gospel. Sing Alleluia. (See page 29)*
*All stand        (adapted from John 1:1-18)*

---

### Gospel

In the beginning
God made a plan.
The plan was Jesus.

Jesus has come to show us the way
to find happiness.

John the Baptist was part of God's plan.
John was sent to help us to get ready,
ready for God's plan,
Jesus.

A. J. McCallen.

---

This is the Gospel of the Lord. **Praise be to you Lord Jesus Christ.**

*All sit*

## Let's chat  (some suggestions)

Do you think God's plan was a good one? Why?
Do you remember the song we sang during Advent?

Let's sing it again.  (See page 14)
If you ever wonder what God is like, just look at Jesus. He's God's son and the image of him.

# Feast of the Holy Family

## Welcome

### Let's praise God
(If celebrating the Introductory Rite, turn to page 28)

*Quietly by yourselves*

### Stop to think

Have you had lots of visitors?
Have you been visiting?
Do people make a fuss of you?

*(If the children have not been visiting at Christmas, encourage them to remember other visits.)*

*When each child has had time to think*

### Share with one another

What happens?
Do they ask you all sorts of questions?
What kind?

'Have you been good?'

'What did Father Christmas bring you?'

'How are you getting on at school?'

'What do you want to be when you grow up?'

'What answer do you give when they ask, "What do you want to be when you grow up?" '

## Light the Gospel candle

*by the crib if you have one*

Today we hear about the time Joseph and Mary took baby Jesus to the Temple. They wanted to say thank you to God for giving them Jesus.

In the Temple they met two people who made a great fuss of Jesus.

*Welcome the Gospel. Sing Alleluia. (See page 29)*

*All stand*        *(adapted from Luke 2:16-21)*

### Gospel

When they came to the Temple
they met an old man called Simeon.
Simeon was a good man and
the Holy Spirit was very close to him.
And as soon as he saw Jesus,
he took him in his arms and said:

'Thank you, God our Father.
Now I am happy to die
for I have seen Jesus,
the Light of the World!'

Then he blessed Joseph and Mary
for they were standing beside him
listening to everything he said,
even though they didn't understand what he meant.

There was also an old woman called Anna in the Temple.
She was always there.
She spent the whole day saying her prayers.
When she saw Jesus
she also thanked God
and told everyone
that Jesus would do many great and wonderful things
when he grew up.

Mary and Joseph did everything they were supposed to do
in the Temple
then they went back to Galilee
and went home to Nazareth.

A. J. McCallen

This is the Gospel of the Lord.
**Praise be to you Lord Jesus Christ.**

*All sit*

## Let's chat *(some suggestions)*

How do you think Simeon and Anna knew who the baby was?
Sing some of your favourite carols.

# God has come to live with us

## Welcome

## Let's sing and say (If celebrating the Introductory Rite, turn to page 28)

*Quietly by yourselves*

## Stop to think

If you could have a dream or a wish come true this year, what would it be?
*(Give the children plenty of time.)*

*When each child has had time to think*

## Share with one another

Share dreams for the year.
Have you ever had a dream come true?
What happened?

## Light the Gospel candle

*by the crib if you have one*
Today we are reminded that the most amazing dream, almost too amazing to come true, did come true!

*Welcome the Gospel. Sing Alleluia. (See page 29)*
*All stand        (adapted from John 1:1-18)*

### Gospel

God is not living in heaven
far away from us.
God is born.
He is living with us.
His name is Jesus.

This is the Gospel of the Lord.

**Praise be to you Lord Jesus Christ.**

*All sit*

## Let's chat *(some suggestions)*

What do you think about that?
Do you think it's an amazing dream come true?
Whose dream do you think it was?

Let's sing. Another carol concert?

# Holy Family

## Welcome

## Let's praise God  *(If celebrating the Introductory Rite, turn to page 28)*

*Quietly by yourselves*

## Stop to think

Have you ever been lost at the shops or on a day out?
How did it happen?
What did you do?
How did you feel?
How did your mum and dad find you?
Did they know where to find you?
What did they say?

*When each child has had time to think*

## Share with one another

This is a common experience for children.

Try to give time to each story.

## Light the Gospel candle

*by the crib if you have one*

Jesus himself got lost when he was twelve years old.

*Welcome the Gospel. Sing Alleluia. (See page 29)*

*All stand*    (adapted from Luke 2:41-52)

## Gospel

On one day of each year
Mary and Joseph went up to
the Temple in Jerusalem.

One year, when Jesus was twelve,
they took him with them as well,
and when everything was finished,
Jesus stayed behind in the city,
and his parents went home without him.

Mary and Joseph thought he was with the
other children,
and they only found out that he had
disappeared when night came.

So they went all the way to Jerusalem
and looked for him everywhere.

After three days of looking
they found him at last in the Temple school
with the other children.
He was listening to the teachers
and asking questions.

All the teachers thought he was very
clever.

Mary was very glad to see him again,
but she asked him what he'd been doing,
and told him how much they'd been
worried.

Jesus told them he was sorry,
but then he said,

"All the same you shouldn't have been
worried,
you should have known
I'd be here in my Father's house."

Mary and Joseph didn't understand what he
meant.

However, he went back to Nazareth again
with them
and he grew up there.
He became tall and strong and wise
for God the Father took good care of him.

A. J. McCallen

This is the Gospel of the Lord.

**Praise be to you Lord Jesus Christ.**

*All sit*

## Let's chat *(some suggestions)*

When we are missing from our family we and they are very sad.
At this time of year lots of families get together.
Is anyone in your family home for Christmas?
Is anyone away this Christmas.
When we are lost all we want to do is find each other.
Now that we are not lost but altogether let's say some thank-you prayers to God for our family.

Thank you for ........................................................................

Thank you for ........................................................................

Thank you for ........................................................................

Enjoy being with your family today and tell them that you love them.

# Jesus is God's Son

## Welcome

## Let's sing and say (If celebrating the Introductory Rite, turn to page 28)

*Quietly by yourselves*

## Stop to think

Before Christmas you had lots of plans for Christmas.

You told people, sometimes one person, sometimes lots of people, sometimes in whispers, sometimes loudly and sometimes you wrote your thoughts in a letter.

Then suddenly all your words, thoughts and dreams came true.
The words become things and happenings.

*When each child has had time to think*

## Share with one another

How did the words (said in so many ways) come alive in actions or events?

## Light the Gospel candle

*by the crib if you have one*
God our Father spoke to people in many ways.
Then God's words, plans and dreams all came true in Jesus.

*Welcome the Gospel. Sing Alleluia.* (See page 29)

*All stand*     (adapted from John 1:1-18)

> ## Gospel
> St John explains it like this,
>
> **"God's word became Jesus."**

This is the Gospel of the Lord.

**Praise be to you Lord Jesus Christ.**

## Let's sing

Sing some of your favourite carols.

# This is my Son!

## Welcome

## Let's sing and say

(If celebrating the Introductory Rite, turn to page 28)

*Quietly by yourselves*

## Stop to think

What kind of new things are happening in school or elsewhere? What new programmes have started on television?
Have you started new sums or a new topic? Have you moved to a new school or new class or a new place in class? Are you beginning to learn anything: how to swim, ride a bike, dance? Have you made a New Year's resolution?

*When each child has had time to think*

## Share with one another

Now that you are getting older what would you like to change about your life? What new starts would you like to make?

## Light the Gospel candle

Lots of people came to the River Jordan to be baptised by John as a sign that they wanted to change their life to live in God's ways. Jesus went to be baptised too as a sign that he was going to begin his great work.

*Welcome the Gospel with a song. (Sing Alleluia page 29)*
*All stand (adapted from Luke 3:21-22)*

### Gospel

Jesus came to be baptised by John.
After he was baptised Jesus went to pray. (Jesus often prayed, and especially before he was going to start something new)

While he was praying everyone heard a voice saying

"This is my Son.
I am pleased with him."

This is the Gospel of the Lord. **Praise be to you Lord Jesus Christ.**

*All sit*

## Let's chat *(some suggestions)*

Do your mum and dad say that they are pleased when they see you making a start on something good? When they see you having a go?

Jesus was just beginning his great work.
We are baptised and at our baptism we promise to help Jesus in his great work; to bring peace and happiness to everyone.
Draw and colour a picture of yourself being baptised.

# Mary, mother of God

*Welcome*

*Let's sing and say* (If celebrating the Introductory Rite, turn to page 28)

*Quietly by yourselves*

## Stop to think

Who chose your name? Why did they choose that name?
Are you called after anyone?
Did it take them a long time to choose it?
Do you have more than one name?

*When each child has had time to think*

## Share with one another

Do you like your name?
What name would you choose for your child?

## Light the Gospel candle *by the crib if you have one*

Today we hear when Jesus was given his name.

*Welcome the Gospel. Sing Alleluia. (See page 29)*

*All stand*      *(adapted from Luke 2:21)*

---

### Gospel

On the eighth day after Mary's baby was born,
she and Joseph named him Jesus.

This was the name the angel suggested when he told
Mary that she was going to have a baby.

---

This is the Gospel of the Lord. **Praise be to you Lord Jesus Christ.**

*All sit*

## Let's chat *(some suggestions)*

Do you like the name Jesus?
Can you remember Jesus' cousin's name?
Can you remember Mary's cousin's name?

Draw and colour a picture of Mary and Joseph naming Jesus and then sing a carol.

# Visitors for Jesus

## Welcome

### Let's sing or say

*(If celebrating the Introductory Rite, turn to page 28)*

*Quietly by yourselves*

### Stop to think

Did you have any visitors over the last few weeks? Did you go visiting? Would you rather visit people or have visitors come to you? Why?

*When each child has had time to think*

### Share with one another

The most important thing about having visitors is that they are made welcome.

### Light the Gospel candle

*by the crib if you have one*

Mary and Joseph had lots of visitors, people they had never met before. Even though they had never met them they made them very welcome. They knew that even though he slept a lot Jesus would want to see everyone and that lots of people they never knew would want to see him.

*Welcome the Gospel. Sing Alleluia.* *(See page 29)*

*All stand* *(adapted from Matthew 2:1-5)*

---

### Gospel

When Jesus was born in Bethlehem
he received a visit from some Wise Men.

First they came to Jerusalem
and they said to King Herod:
"Where will we find the baby
who is the king of the Jews?"

King Herod didn't like this
(he didn't want anyone to be king except himself!)
But he asked the priest and the teachers
if they knew anything about it,
and they said:

"A long time ago
God spoke to the people of Bethlehem like this:

"I promise you,
the Great King will be born in
Bethlehem.

He will look after you
like a shepherd who looks after his sheep.

He will take care of you.
He will never let you down
for he will be the King of the World.'

So King Herod sent his visitors off to Bethlehem.
"You find the baby", he said.
"Then come back
and tell me where I can find him,
and I will go and see him as well."

So the Wise Men went to Bethlehem
and they found Jesus there
with his mother, Mary,
and they gave him their presents.

But they didn't trust King Herod
and they didn't go back to him.

A. J. McCallen

This is the Gospel of the Lord.

**Praise be to you Lord Jesus Christ.**

*All sit*

## Let's chat *(some suggestions)*

What do you think about what happened?
Which is the best part?
Would Mary and Joseph be surprised by their visitors?
Would Herod be surprised?
Why didn't the Wise Men trust Herod?
Draw or colour a picture of the three visitors.

# *Lent*

## *Six Sundays before Easter*

The season of Lent begins on Ash Wednesday. Wearing ashes that day is a sign that we are sorry for our sins and that we are going to try to become better people. It sums up the spirit of the whole season.

The season begins by recalling the forty days Jesus spent in the desert preparing for his ministry by fasting and praying. The readings call us to 'Yes' to God's will and 'No' to our selfish ways so that we too might be his ministers. We do this so that the glory of God is revealed.

Traditionally we give more time to:

## Prayer

No special words are needed in prayer – all that matters is that our words come from the heart. Prayer is really a time for consciously being in Jesus' company.
We can talk to Him as we might any special friend. Persuade the children to pray for a short time each day. The picture below may help them to focus their attention on Jesus.

## Fasting

There are no fast laws for children. Keep in mind that the spirit of fasting is to help us to become less self-indulgent not hungry; being hungry is not a virtue. Try and help the children to find ways to be less greedy, less selfish.

## Almsgiving

A great deal of fund raising will be happening in the children's schools.
It may be an opportunity for forming some kind of link.

Make a money box (see page 47).
If it's too difficult for the younger children, paint and decorate an empty Smartie tube. It can take 75p in 1p coins to fill.

Twenty pence coins fit too!

• *Keep in mind Mother's Day is always the 4th Sunday of Lent.*

## LENT ACTIVITY (1)

*Prepare flowers for the Easter season*

Give each child a copy of this paper pattern.

Each week they can write on one of the petals some secret good deed and fold the petal over the centre of the flower. On Easter Sunday float the paper flower on a bowl of water, the petals will unfold to reveal all their secret goodness to the world! When dry they can be added to the Easter Garden.

# LENT ACTIVITY (2)

## *Lent savings box*

How to make your savings box:

- copy this shape on some light cardboard:

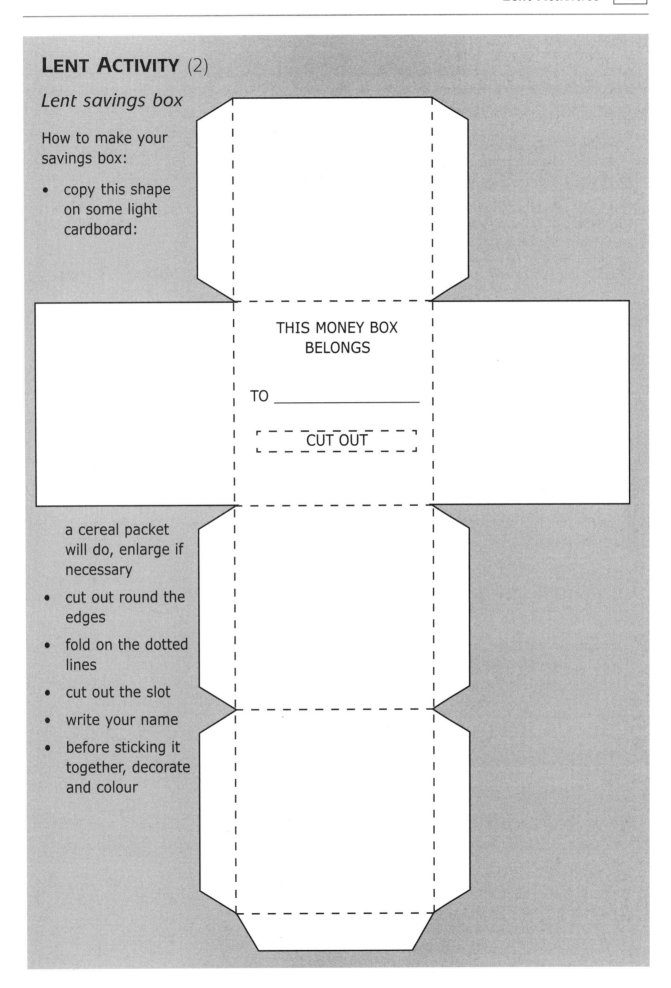

THIS MONEY BOX
BELONGS

TO _____

CUT OUT

a cereal packet will do, enlarge if necessary

- cut out round the edges
- fold on the dotted lines
- cut out the slot
- write your name
- before sticking it together, decorate and colour

## INTRODUCTORY RITE

## Sign of the Cross

## Penitential Rite

Our friend Jesus,
Help me to be good,
to do the things and say the things
all good children should,

And if I sometime slip a bit
and do get out of hand,
Then please, my friend Jesus
remind me that you always understand

that it isn't always easy
to be a good as good can be.
But I am getting better Lord,
'cause you are helping me.

## Song – Lord, have mercy (Israeli Mass)

Israeli folk melody
Adapted by Anthony Hamson

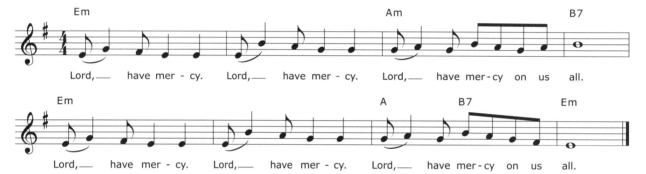

Lord,— have mer-cy. Lord,— have mer-cy. Lord,— have mer-cy on us all.

Lord,— have mer-cy. Lord,— have mer-cy. Lord,— have mer-cy on us all.

Christ, have mercy. Christ, have mercy.
Christ, have mercy on us all.
Christ, have mercy. Christ, have mercy.
Christ, have mercy on us all.

Lord, have mercy. Lord, have mercy.
Lord, have mercy on us all.
Lord, have mercy. Lord, have mercy.
Lord, have mercy on us all.

## Opening Prayer

*Let us pray*

Father,
Help us to understand
how to be good
to other people,
so that we can be
just like Jesus.
We ask this as his friends.
Amen.

*End of Introductory Rite, turn to Sunday text* ➤

## Gospel Acclamation – We have come to hear the Lord

(To the tune 'Merrily we roll along')

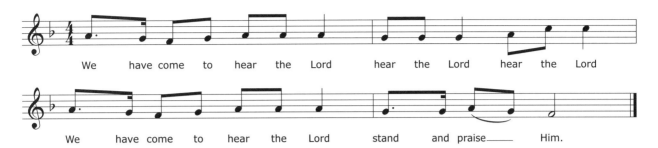

We have come to hear the Lord,
    hear the Lord,
    hear the Lord.
We have come to hear the Lord,
    stand and praise him.

*Alternative Gospel Acclamation*

## Glory and praise to you

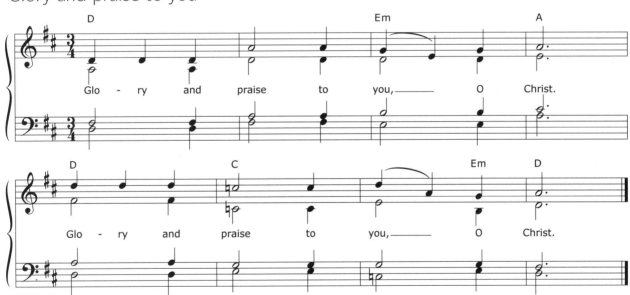

© McCrimmon Publishing Co. Ltd.

Glory and praise to you, O Christ.
Glory and praise to you, O Christ.

**LENT**

| | |
|---|---|
| **Year A** | begins on page 50 |
| **Year B** | begins on page 57 |
| **Year C** | begins on page 62 |

# Saying no

## Welcome

## Let's sing and say
(If celebrating the Introductory Rite, turn to page 48)

*Quietly by yourselves*
## Stop to think
What makes it so difficult to be good?

- People tease and torment you?
- People keep getting in your way?
- People keep touching your things, sometimes taking them?
- People call you names?

*When each child has had time to think*
## Share with one another
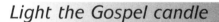
What annoys you the most? What really makes you angry so that you lose your temper?
*(Leaders tell the children what makes it hard for you to be good.)*

## Light the Gospel candle
Sometimes we think, if we didn't have all these people around us, pestering us, we could be really good. All we need to do is to get away and be on our own.
Do you think that would work?

This week we hear that Jesus went into the desert on his own. He didn't go there to get away from people pestering him. He went to spend time thinking and praying to God our Father. It still wasn't easy to be good.

*Welcome the Gospel with a song. (Gospel acclamations – see page 49)*

*All stand  (adapted from Matthew 4:1-11)*

## Gospel

Jesus went into the desert for forty days
to think and pray
and during that time he didn't have anything to eat!

Jesus didn't find this easy to do.
He saw the stones
which he could make into bread.
But Jesus chose not to
because he knew God our Father
had other things for him to do.

Then Jesus climbed a mountain.
He could see for miles and miles.
He could see many countries
and Jesus knew that he could make himself
the King of all this land.
But he chose not to
because he knew God our Father is the only King.

Then leaving the desert
he went to Jerusalem to the Temple.
He climbed to the top.
He knew that he didn't have to climb down again.
If he jumped from the roof
God would save him from being hurt.
He chose not to.
Jesus said "It's not right to test God's love."

Jesus knew that God loved him very much
though life was not always easy for him.

This is the Gospel of the Lord. **Praise be to you Lord Jesus Christ.**

*All sit*

## Let's chat *(some suggestions)*

Getting away from everyone doesn't make doing what's right any easier, does it?
We can still be tempted to do the wrong thing.
How many times was Jesus tempted?
What did he choose to do each time?
Was it easy for him?
What would you have done if you were Jesus?

Each day we have the choice – to do what's right or to do what's wrong.
We have to choose all on our own (though Jesus will help us).

This means that we have to become our own boss. We must learn to "boss" ourselves.
It isn't easy to do. We would always rather spoil ourselves.

The choice is ours!

# This is a wonderful place

*Welcome*

*Let's sing and say* *(If celebrating the Introductory Rite, turn to page 48)*

*Quietly by yourselves*

## Stop to think

Have you ever been taken to a special place where other people don't usually go?

- The back of a shop?
- Into the teacher's staff room?
- Inside your mum/dad's office?
- Where?

*When each child has had time to think*

## Share with one another

Where did you go? Did it make you feel special? Why were you chosen?
Why did you go? What happened?

## Light the Gospel candle

Jesus took three friends to a special place. They saw some wonderful things.
On their way home Jesus asked them to keep it a secret for a while.

*Welcome the Gospel with a song* (Gospel acclamations – page 49)

*All stand (adapted from Matthew 17:1-9)*

## Gospel

Jesus took Peter, James and John up to the top of a high mountain.
They went there to pray.

While they were there two men appeared (Elijah and Moses) they were talking to Jesus.

Jesus looked absolutely radiant!
He looked wonderful.

Peter said to Jesus,
"This is a wonderful place, let's put up three tents."

Peter hadn't finished speaking when everywhere clouded over and became dark. Then they all heard a voice from the cloud saying,
"This is my Son, the chosen one, listen to him."

When they looked again the two men had gone and they were alone with Jesus so they went home.

On the way home Jesus said,
"Don't tell anyone until after I have risen from the dead."

This is the Gospel of the Lord. **Praise be to you Lord Jesus Christ.**

## Let's chat *All sit (some suggestions)*

Do you wish that you had been there? What would you have done?
Why do you think Peter wanted to put up tents?
What was God our Father telling us? Why? Do you think the friends were surprised that Jesus asked them to keep it a secret for a while? Why do you think Jesus said that?
They did keep the secret. Could you have kept it?

# The woman at the well

## Welcome

## Let's sing and say   *(If celebrating the Introductory Rite, turn to page 48)*

*Quietly by yourselves*

## Stop to think

Have you ever been to a cafe and noticed who is talking to who?

People sometimes keep themselves to themselves, other times they soon get talking to each other.

Does your mum always start talking to someone or does someone always seem to start talking to her? Do you join in or are you too shy?

*When each child has had time to think*

## Share with one another

Share experiences of meeting people, being shy and 'breaking the ice'. *(Explain the saying)*

Once people have begun to talk they soon find out a great deal about each other.

Have you ever met anyone interesting?

## Light the Gospel candle

Today we hear about a lady Jesus once met at a well. She was very surprised that Jesus spoke to her. Where Jesus came from the people didn't talk to people from the place this lady came from!

*Welcome the Gospel with a song  (Gospel acclamations – page 49)*

*All stand  (adapted from John 4:4-5, 19-26, 39-42)*

## Gospel

Jesus was on a journey when he became tired and thirsty so he stopped at a well called "Jacob's Well".

A woman came to the well with her bucket to collect some water.
Jesus asked her for a drink.
She was very surprised!

They soon began to talk to each other.
They quickly found out a lot about each other too.

When the woman realised that she was talking to Jesus, the great King!
she ran to tell her friends.

Her friends believed her.
Jesus stayed in their town for a while and they all met him for themselves.

This is the Gospel of the Lord. **Praise be to you Lord Jesus Christ.**

*All sit*

## Let's chat *(some suggestions)*

How do you think the woman felt when she realised who she was talking to?

One of the wonderful things about Jesus is that he talks to anyone, anywhere and anytime.

You can talk to Jesus anytime and anywhere.

# Help us to see

## Welcome

## Let's sing and say   *(If celebrating the Introductory Rite, turn to page 48)*

*Quietly by yourselves*

## Stop to think

Do you know anyone who is blind? What would it be like?

*When each child has had time to think*

## Share with one another

What's it like?
Even though we can see, in some ways we are blind. We don't see what's under our nose!
Have you ever been looking for something and it was in front of you all the time?
*(Explain the saying 'Can't see the wood for the trees'.)*

## Light the Gospel candle

Jesus helps us to see, see things that go unnoticed. He can even help the blind to see!

*Welcome the Gospel with a song  (Gospel acclamations – page 49)*

*All stand  (adapted from John 9:1, 6-9)*

## Gospel

Jesus was walking along when he saw a blind man.
The man had been blind since he was born.

Jesus bent down and spat on the ground so that he could make a paste from the dust.
He put the paste on the man's eyes and then told him to wash it off.

The man did as he was told and when he had finished washing he could see.

The neighbours couldn't believe it.
"It's not the same man," they said.
"It's someone who just looks like him!"

Then the man who had been blind said, "It is me!"

This is the Gospel of the Lord.

**Praise be to you Lord Jesus Christ.**

*All sit*

## Let's chat   *(some suggestions)*

What do you think happened next?
What would the man want to see first of all?
What other things does Jesus help us to see?

Is there anything you haven't noticed about your mum?
Today is the day to notice and say thanks.

# Anyone who believes in me will have new life

*Welcome*

*Let's sing and say*

*(If celebrating the Introductory Rite, turn to page 48)*

*Quietly by yourselves*

## Stop to think

Have you ever watched anything change, get a new life:

- a tadpole into a frog?
- a caterpillar into a butterfly?
- an egg into a chick?
- a bulb into a flower?
- a bean or seed into a plant?

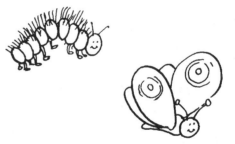

*When each child has had time to think*

## Share with one another

What have you seen?

It's quite amazing to see anything change from one thing to another?

Sometimes it's hard to know what will happen. Can you tell the difference between a bulb and an onion?

Can you tell the difference between bulbs?

We know what changes into what and we trust it will happen, but it can still be a surprise and it can still amaze us.

## Light the Gospel candle

Jesus is telling us this week that we too will have a new life because we believe in him and trust him.

*Welcome the Gospel with a song.  (Gospel acclamations – page 49)*

*All stand  (adapted from John 11:1-44)*

### Gospel

 Lazarus and his two sisters Martha and Mary lived in Bethany.
They were great friends of Jesus.

Lazarus became very ill.
Martha and Mary sent for Jesus.
Two days later Jesus went to see them.

When Jesus arrived Martha came out to meet him and said,
  "If you had been here my brother wouldn't have died."

Jesus said,
  "Anyone who believes in me will have new life."

Martha and Mary believed Jesus.

He went with Martha and Mary to where Lazarus was buried.

He closed his eyes and prayed.

Afterwards he said,

  "Thank you Father, you always help me, I want everyone to know that you have sent me."

Then he said, "Come out Lazarus!"

Lazarus came out alive.

This is the Gospel of the Lord.

**Praise be to you Lord Jesus Christ.**

*All sit*

### Let's chat  *(some suggestions)*

If you had been there would you have believed just like Martha and Mary?

Would you believe just the same or more after you had seen Lazarus?
Do you believe that Jesus will one day give you new life? Perhaps this week you could show a new part of your character and surprise someone. What could you do?

# The time has come

## Welcome

## Let's sing and say

*(If celebrating the Introductory Rite, turn to page 48)*

*Quietly by yourselves*

## Stop to think

Do you know what a diet is?
Do you know anyone who is going on a diet?
Why are they dieting?

*When each child has had time to think*

## Share with one another

At this time of year lots of people start to change their ways.
They start to diet, exercise more or try to give up smoking.
We all ate too much at Christmas and haven't stopped spoiling ourselves since.
If we don't stop and put things right, goodness knows what kind of people we will become!
Probably very selfish.

## Light the Gospel candle

Jesus knows that selfish people make an unhappy world.
The time has come to stop and change our ways.

*Welcome the Gospel with a song. (Gospel acclamations – page 49)*

*All stand (adapted from Mark 1:14-15)*

### Gospel

After Jesus had left the desert where he had done a lot of thinking he said,
"The time has come!
Change your selfish ways.
I have come to help you."

This is the Gospel of the Lord.

**Praise be to you Lord Jesus Christ.**

*All sit*

## Let's chat (some suggestions)

Can you think of any selfish things that people do?
Choose two unselfish things that you could do for someone this week.
Draw them so that you won't forget.
You will make two people very happy this week.
Perhaps you might draw some pictures about what you plan to do.

I will...

# Jesus is certainly God's son

## Welcome

## Let's sing and say *(If celebrating the Introductory Rite, turn to page 48)*

*Quietly by yourselves*

## Stop to think

Has your mum ever told you some exciting news and then said, "Don't tell anyone yet as it's a secret for the moment"? Did you keep the secret or did you tell a friend?
How long did you have to keep the secret for?

*When each child has had time to think*

## Share with one another

Can you share your secret now? What was the good news?
Why do you think the news had to be kept secret?
Why did your mum tell you? Are you any good at keeping secrets?

## Light the Gospel candle

This week some of Jesus' friends had some great news but they couldn't tell anyone because Jesus asked them to keep it a secret for a while.

*Welcome the Gospel with a song. (Gospel acclamations – page 49)*
*All stand (adapted from Mark 9:2-10)*

### Gospel

Jesus, Peter, James and John went up a mountain to pray. While they were there, they saw Jesus talking to two men. (Elijah and Moses) Jesus looked absolutely radiant.
He looked wonderful.
Peter said to Jesus,
"This is a wonderful place, let's put up tents."
Peter hadn't finished speaking when everywhere clouded over and became dark.

Then they heard a voice from the cloud saying,

"This is my Son,
 the Chosen One,
 listen to Him."

When they looked again the two men had gone and they were alone with Jesus.

On the way home Jesus said,
 "Don't tell anyone, keep it a secret for the moment, you can tell after I have died and come alive again."

The friends didn't understand what Jesus was talking about, but they promised to keep the secret.

This is the Gospel of the Lord. **Praise be to you Lord Jesus Christ.**

*All sit*

## Let's chat *(some suggestions)*

Could you keep it a secret?
Do you understand what Jesus meant when he said "You can tell after I have died and come alive again"?

Why didn't his friends understand?
They must have been special friends to have been told such a wonderful thing.
This week could you do something wonderful and keep it a secret?

# God's way

## Welcome

## Let's sing and say *(If celebrating the Introductory Rite, turn to page 48)*

*Quietly by yourselves*

## Stop to think

Have you got a special place, somewhere you love to be or somewhere you keep your special things? Perhaps you have a den?

*After each child has had time to think*

## Share with one another

Where is your special place?
Has anyone ever come along and spoilt it? How?
We all have some place which is important, quite sacred to us.
People can spoil these places by not treating them properly.

## Light the Gospel candle

Jesus got angry with some people who were spoiling the Temple. They were spoiling it by using it to buy and sell things and to cheat people. Jesus doesn't like people to be cheated and he certainly doesn't like it being done in his church.

*Welcome the Gospel with a song. (Gospel acclamations – page 49)*

*All stand* (adapted from John 2:13-25)

## Gospel

Jesus went to the Temple in Jerusalem.
It was a very special place.
When he arrived he found all sorts of people who were buying and selling things.

They were trying to see who could make the most money and some people were cheating, even stealing.

Jesus was angry, he threw them all out shouting,
"Don't make my Father's house into a market."

This is the Gospel of the Lord.
**Praise be to you Lord Jesus Christ.**

*All sit*

## Let's chat *(some suggestions)*

Why was Jesus angry? Was it just about the way they were using the Temple?
What else was Jesus upset about?

How does Jesus want us to behave in church? How does Jesus want us to behave with each other?
What sort of things spoil your church?

# Walk in the light

## Welcome

*Let's sing or say* (If celebrating the Introductory Rite, turn to page 48)

*Quietly by yourselves*

## Stop to think

Are you sometimes frightened by the dark? We all are. (Just in case some claim to be braver than they really are.) Do you like mum to leave the hall/landing light on at night? Do you like to have a torch with you in the dark?

*When each child has had time to think*

## Share with one another

(Many will not like to admit being frightened of the dark)
What do you like about the light? What do you like about the dark? Mum leaves a light on so that we won't be afraid and no harm can come to us. If we need to get up we won't lose our way or fall over.

## Light the Gospel candle

God loves us so much that he sent his son Jesus into the world to be our light. With Jesus no harm can come to us.

*Welcome the Gospel with a song. (Gospel acclamations – see page 49)*
*All stand (adapted from John 3:14-21)*

---

### Gospel

One night when everyone was in bed and all was quiet a man came to see Jesus.
His name was Nicodemus.

Nicodemus believed in Jesus and wanted to know more about him.

Jesus told Nicodemus God loved the world so much that he sent his only Son to the world to be the light.

---

This is the Gospel of the Lord. **Praise be to you Lord Jesus Christ.**

*All sit*

## Let's chat (some suggestions)

Nicodemus went to see Jesus at night because he didn't want anyone to know that he believed in Jesus. He was worried about what people might say.

Sometimes we are like that, we do things out of sight hoping that no one will notice, especially if it is something wrong.
But if we are doing what's right, then we shouldn't mind who sees. Do you think Nicodemus was right to go at night?

*Give each child some mustard or cress seeds to plant. Ask them what size they think the plant will be by next week.*

# Put yourself out

## Welcome

## Let's sing and say   (If celebrating the Introductory Rite, turn to page 48)

*Quietly by yourselves*

## Stop to think

*(Give each child another seed)*

Do you remember the seeds you planted last week?
How big do you think they have grown?

*When each child has had time to think*

## Share with one another

After all the guesses bring out the plants. Who was right?
Who would have imagined that such a big plant was inside such a small seed?
If we left the seeds in the packet would they have grown? What did we have to do?
It wasn't very pleasant sticking our fingers into dark, wet soil, but it was the only way the plants would have grown.

*(Keep the plants for your Easter Garden)*

## Light the Gospel candle

Sometimes we have to do unpleasant, uncomfortable
things for good things to happen.

*Welcome the Gospel with a song.* (Gospel acclamations page 49)
*All stand (adapted from John 12:23-28)*

## Gospel

Jesus was troubled, he knew that the time had come.
He had a job to do.

He wondered about it and said,
"Even though it's difficult and unpleasant I must do it.
This is the job my Father has asked of me."

Jesus remembered the seeds and said to his friends
"If you plant a seed, it grows and you can eat it, but if you want it to have a comfortable life in a packet it never grows. What use is a seed in a packet?"

This is the Gospel of the Lord. **Praise be to you Lord Jesus Christ.**

*All sit*

## Let's chat   *(some suggestions)*

If we never put ourselves out for others, what use are we?
What could we do to put ourselves out for someone this week?

# Jesus is tempted

## Welcome

## Let's sing and say

*(If celebrating the Introductory Rite, turn to page 48)*

*Quietly by yourselves*

## Stop to think

Do you know anyone who is going on a diet? Why?
What are your family and friends planning to do this Lent?
What have you chosen to do?

*When each child has had time to think*

## Share Lenten resolutions

*(Encourage simple, achievable resolutions for a short period of time, e.g. a day each week or a week at a time, rather than all Lent. Failure will discourage the children).*

We need this time to sort ourselves out.
We ate too much and spoilt ourselves at
Christmas and we haven't really stopped.
If we carry on thinking about ourselves so
much, we will forget about others.
This isn't what God our Father wants at all!
We need time to stop and think.

## Light the Gospel candle

Jesus took time out to stop and think. He really wanted to know what God our Father wanted him to do.

*Welcome the Gospel with a song. (Gospel acclamations – see page 49)*

*All stand*     (adapted from Luke 4:1-13)

## Gospel

 Jesus went into the desert for forty days to think and pray and during that time he didn't have anything to eat!

Jesus didn't find this easy to do. He saw the stones which he could make into bread. But Jesus chose not to because he knew God our Father had other things for him to do.

Then Jesus climbed a mountain. He could see for miles and miles. He could see many countries and Jesus knew that he could make himself the King of all this land. But he chose not to because he knew God our Father is the only King.

Then leaving the desert he went to Jerusalem to the Temple. He climbed to the top. He knew that he didn't have to climb down again. If he jumped from the roof God would save him from being hurt. He chose not to. Jesus said
   "it's not right to test God's love."

Jesus knew that God loved him very much though life was not always easy for him.

This is the Gospel of the Lord. **Praise be to you Lord Jesus Christ.**

*All sit*

## Let's chat *(some suggestions)*

Was it easy for Jesus in the desert?
Do you think that he might have wanted to go home?
What would you have done?
Jesus didn't give up even though he was tempted. He wanted to do what was right.
This Lent there will be lots of times when we want to give up, so let's ask for Jesus' help.

> **Jesus you prayed for forty days**
>    **that was a long time.**
> **And you didn't give up**
> **even though you sometimes found it**
>    **hard to do!**

> **Help me today not to give up**
> **when I find it difficult to keep my**
>    **lenten promise.**
> **It was hard for you, it will be hard**
>    **for me.**
> **I know you will help me.**

Perhaps we could pray each day for forty seconds.

Forty seconds last this long...
*(Leaders give the children some idea how long forty seconds lasts).*

Who can pray for that long each day?

# A glorious moment

## Welcome

## Let's sing and say   *(If celebrating the Introductory Rite, turn to page 48)*

*Quietly by yourselves*

## Stop to think

Have you ever climbed to the top of a mountain or to the top of a building, looked out and thought, wow!

*When each child has had time to think*

## Share with one another

Share experiences of seeing sights and saying 'wow!' (TV or otherwise). Explain to the children the phrase 'took my breath away'. When we see wonderful sights we often think: "Isn't God amazing?" We want to keep the moment for ever; sometimes we take photographs to help us remember.

## Light the Gospel candle

Today we hear about a wonderful moment in Jesus' life that took Peter, James and John's breath away.

*Welcome the Gospel with a song.  (Gospel acclamations page 49)*

*All stand*     *(adapted from Luke 9:28-36)*

---

### Gospel

Jesus, Peter, James and John went up a mountain to pray. While they were there they saw Jesus talking to two men. (Elijah and Moses)

Jesus looked absolutely radiant. He looked wonderful.

Peter said to Jesus "This is a wonderful place, let's put up tents."

Peter hadn't finished speaking when everywhere clouded over and became dark. Then they heard a voice from the cloud saying
"This is my Son the chosen one. Listen to him."

The two men had gone and they were alone with Jesus so they went home.

---

This is the Gospel of the Lord. **Praise be to you Lord Jesus Christ.**

*All sit*

## Let's chat   *(some suggestions)*

What a wonderful day!
Which was the best part?
Do you wish you had been there?
What would you have done, said?

Should the apostles (Jesus' friends) have been frightened? Why?
Who spoke?
What was God trying to tell us?

Try and think of something you could do to make someone say, 'that's wonderful'.

# One more chance

## *Welcome*

## *Let's sing and say* (If celebrating the Introductory Rite, turn to page 48)

*Quietly by yourselves*

## *Stop to think*

Are you often late? Does your mum say 'hurry up or we'll be late,' or 'get a move on or we'll be too late.' Does she often say it? When does she say it?

*When each child has had time to think*

## *Share with one another*

Share experiences of being just on time. Share experiences of being just too late. Whenever we find ourselves being late or rushing we say 'Next time we will start earlier, we will plan and prepare properly.'

## *Light the Gospel candle*

In this week's Gospel it would seem that the 'next time' for a fruit tree has almost run out. However, it's given another chance, a last chance.

*Welcome the Gospel with a song. (Gospel acclamations page 49)*

*All stand (adapted from Luke 13:6-9)*

---

### Gospel

Jesus told this story.

One day a man went to pick fruit from his fruit tree.
But when he got to the tree
he saw that the tree had no fruit.
He went to the gardener and said
   "We've had this tree for three years
   and it hasn't grown a single piece of fruit."

Then the man said,
"I give up, cut it down
it's taking up useful space."

The gardener said
"Let's wait till next year,
I'll look after it and manure it;
maybe next year it will have fruit,
if not then you can cut it down."

---

This is the Gospel of the Lord. **Praise be to you Lord Jesus Christ.**

*All sit*

## *Let's chat* (some suggestions)

What do you think Jesus is trying to tell us?

Let's pray: Jesus,
we don't know where the time goes.

Whole days have passed by unnoticed;
we can't believe we are almost
half way through Lent;

we have missed so many chances
to help others.

Please help us to stop and think,
to act now,
not to leave till tomorrow
what we can do today.

Thank you for another day,
another chance.

# Coming home

## Welcome

## Let's sing and say
*(If celebrating the Introductory Rite, turn to page 48)*

*Quietly by yourselves*
## Stop to think

We all love our mums but sometimes we get angry and say that we are going to run away. Have you ever done this? Have you ever lost your mum in a crowd?

*When each child has had time to think*
## Share with one another

When you ran away or got lost did you miss your mum?
How did you feel?
Were you glad to be home?
What did you do and say when you found your mum!

## Light the Gospel candle

This week we hear about a boy who left home because he had grown up. He came back home when he got in trouble.

*Welcome the Gospel with a song. (Gospel acclamations page 49)*

*All stand (adapted from Luke 15:11-24)*

## Gospel

One day Jesus told his friends this story.

There was once a farmer who had two sons. The younger son came to his father and said:

"Isn't it about time that you gave me my share of the farm?"

So the father gave him his share of the money.
A few days later, the boy packed his bags and left home.
He went a long way away and he had a good time, but he wasted all his money, until at last he didn't even have enough to buy something to eat.
So he had to get a job on a farm feeding the pigs and he was so hungry he would have eaten the pig-swill if he could have got it!

Then he began to think. "What a fool I am!" he said to himself.
"Even the men who only work for my Father have as much as they want to eat. And here am I, starving to death.
I know I have hurt God and I've hurt my Father but I'm going back home.
I'll tell my Father I am sorry and I'll ask him to give me a job as a workman because I'm not good enough to be called his son anymore."

So he went home again and his Father saw him coming.
He felt sorry for the boy and ran out to meet him and made him welcome.

The boy began to say, "I have done wrong..."
But his Father did not wait for him to finish.
He told his servants to get out some good clothes for the boy and to get a meal ready.

"I thought I had lost my boy," he said, "I thought he was dead.
But now he is alive again, and I have found him once more."

A. J. McCallen

This is the Gospel of the Lord.

**Praise be to you Lord Jesus Christ.**

*All sit*

## Let's chat *(some suggestions)*

Do you think he was glad to be home?
What do you think was the first thing that he did?
The boy came home because he was hungry and having a bad time. Jesus loves us to turn to him always, especially when we are having a bad time.

*For older children:*
This week why not go to the Sacrament of Reconciliation.
Talk to Father about your troubles and your bad times.
Tell him about the things you do well and the things you want to change. He might have an idea or two to help you.

# Telling tales

## Welcome

## Let's sing and say  *(If celebrating the Introductory Rite, turn to page 48)*

*Quietly by yourselves*

## Stop to think

Have you ever heard the song      'Tell tale, tit.
Your tongue shall be slit
and all the little dogs in town
shall have a little bit.'

It isn't a very nice song. When do people say it?

*When each child has had time to think*

## Share with one another

*Discuss 'telling tales'.*

Nobody likes a tell-tale, someone who wants to get us into trouble.
What do people say when they are going to tell a tale?
"I'm going to tell Miss/Sir" "I'm telling on you"
"Ah... I'm going to tell Mum"

*Explain to the children the saying, 'People in glass houses shouldn't throw stones'.*

## Light the Gospel candle

This week we hear about the time when Jesus was interrupted by tell-tales.

*Welcome the Gospel with a song. (Gospel acclamations page 49)*

*All stand*      *(adapted from John 8:1-11)*

## Gospel

 One day Jesus was busy teaching in the Temple.

A group of people came in bringing a woman with them. They made her stand up in front of everybody and everybody looked at her. They said to Jesus, "This woman has been doing bad things, the rules say that she should be stoned as her punishment. What do you think?" They really wanted to catch Jesus out.

Jesus bent down and started to write with his finger
then he looked up and said.
   "If there is anyone among you
    who has never done anything bad,
     then they can throw the first stone."

Then Jesus bent down to write again.
One by one they went away.
Jesus said to the woman
   "Has anyone thrown a stone at you?"
   She said "No."

Then Jesus said,
   "Neither will I,
    you are forgiven,
    go home and try to be good."

This is the Gospel of the Lord.
**Praise be to you Lord Jesus Christ.**

*All sit*

## Let's chat *(some suggestions)*

What do you think Jesus wrote on the ground with his finger?
What do you think he thought of the people who brought the woman to him?
What do you think he thought of the woman?
What do you think about them both?

This week don't tell tales. Be ready to forgive others.

# *Hosanna!*

## Welcome

The material for today concentrates on the first Gospel (Blessing of the Palms) rather than the passion. They will likely have heard the passion told in school and there will be an opportunity for the children to hear it on Good Friday. If they don't hear it today don't worry. We may do more harm than good to children's faith by giving them too much too soon.

## Let's sing and say

(If celebrating the Introductory Rite, turn to page 48)

*Quietly by yourselves*

## Stop to think

If the children have been part of the blessing of palms and the procession ask: What was it like in the crowd? Could you see anything? What could you see?
What could you hear?
Did you enjoy receiving your palm?

*If not ask:*

Have you ever been stuck in a crowd? When, what for?
Is it exciting being part of a crowd greeting someone?

*When each child has had time to think*

## Share with one another

What happens when someone everyone wants to see and talk to comes into your school playground?

## Light the Gospel candle

*Welcome the Gospel with a song.  (Gospel acclamations page 49)*

*All stand  (adapted from Luke 19:28-40)*

### Gospel

When they arrived at the Olive Hill,
Jesus said to two of his friends,
   "If you go into that village over there,
   you will find a donkey and its foal, just as you go in.
   Untie them and bring them here.
   If anyone asks you who they are for,
   tell them they're for me,
   and I will send them back as soon as I can."

So off they went
and brought back the donkey and the foal,
with their coats spread over the animals' backs,
and Jesus then got on.
Some people even put their coats on the ground
in front of Jesus.
Others cut branches off the trees
and put them on the ground for Jesus to ride over.

There were lots of people,
walking in front of Jesus
and walking behind him,
and they all shouted
   "Hosanna, Hosanna!
   Blessed is he who comes
   in the name of the Lord.
   Hosanna, Hosanna!"

A. J. McCallen

This is the Gospel of the Lord.

**Praise be to you Lord Jesus Christ.**

*All sit*

## Let's chat  *(some suggestions)*

Some of the local leaders complained that Jesus' followers were getting too excited.

They were worried that they were getting out of hand.
Do you think they were?

The leader told Jesus to calm his friends down. Have you enjoyed waving your palm?
Do you need to calm down?

This might be a happy day but it's the beginning of a sad week which has a very happy ending.

# *Easter*

## *From Easter to Trinity Sunday*

This is the season for rejoicing in Jesus' new life and his victory over death. The celebrations last for seven weeks, finishing with Pentecost and Trinity Sunday.

## Paschal Candle

This should be at the centre of the celebrations. It symbolises Jesus coming alive after his death. We too will have new life in heaven. Show the children the Paschal Candle in your Church and remind them that as well as being lit during Easter it is lit at baptism. It was lit for their baptism. Their baptism was special.

Paschal candles can be easily made with rolled paper.

The date of the year is usually written around the cross.

## EASTER ACTIVITIES (1)

### Easter garden

We can help children rejoice in new life by giving them experiences of growing seeds, etc.

City children often miss the signs of spring and new life around them.

Try making an Easter garden as illustrated. Keep the areas around

the cross bare and fill the area around the tomb with as many plants and flowers as possible. Let the children plant seeds in egg cups – they will delight in watching them grow.

## EASTER ACTIVITIES (2)

### Easter Eggs

Eggs are a clear symbol of new life (perhaps use real egg shells for planting seeds.)

Most children love to eat their Easter eggs as soon as they are given them while others prefer to savour them, keeping them for weeks. Their motivation often has less to do with celebrating the whole of the Easter season and more to do with teasing sisters and brothers or health conscious parents. However by keeping them so long such children remind us all that the Easter season does not finish on Easter Monday. Try and have an Easter egg on the holy table throughout the season.

## INTRODUCTORY RITE

## Sign of the Cross

## Penitential Rite

> May almighty God
> have mercy on us,
> forgive us,
> and bring us to everlasting life.
> Amen.

## Gloria – Rise and Shine
Traditional

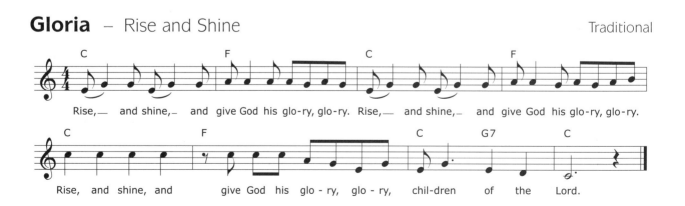

Rise,— and shine,— and give God his glo-ry, glo-ry. Rise,— and shine,— and give God his glo-ry, glo-ry.

Rise, and shine, and give God his glo - ry, glo - ry, chil-dren of the Lord.

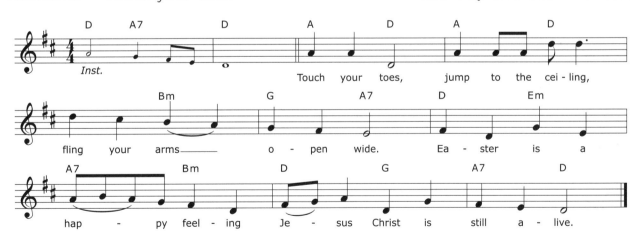

## Opening Prayer

*Let us pray*

Father,
As we celebrate
the new life of Jesus,
Help us to be new
in our love for you
and others.

We ask this as friends of
your son Jesus.
Amen.

*End of Introductory Rite, turn to Sunday text*  ➤

## Gospel Acclamation – One, two, three, four, five
Traditional
(Sing to the tune 'Once I caught a fish alive')

One two three four five Our friend Je - sus is a - live

six sev - en eight nine ten Yes he will come back a - gain.

One, two, three, four, five,
my friend Jesus is alive.
Six, seven, eight, nine, ten,
yes he will come back again.

*Alternative: - Touch your toes*
Kevin Mayhew and John Rombaut

Touch your toes, jump to the cei - ling,

fling your arms o - pen wide. Ea - ster is a

hap - py feel - ing Je - sus Christ is still a - live.

© McCrimmon Publishing Co. Ltd.

Touch your toes,
jump to the ceiling
fling your arms open wide.
Easter is a happy feeling
Jesus Christ is still alive.

*Repeat a second time with actions*

| EASTER | |
| --- | --- |
| **Year A** | begins on page 76 |
| **Year B** | begins on page 85 |
| **Year C** | begins on page 91 |

# Jesus is alive

## Welcome

## Let's praise

> **GLORY** be to the Father
> and to the Son
> and to the Holy Spirit, Amen.

This is the greatest day of the year.

## Let's sing and say

(If celebrating the Introductory Rite, turn to page 74)

*Quietly by yourselves*

## Stop to think

Look around the room and try and think of an impossible task for me or for anyone else here this morning. When you have thought of one ask me or someone else to test it out.

*When each child has had time to think*

## Share with one another

Are you ready? What's your test?

*(Without too much chaos, if that's possible, test out the impossible and good luck!)*

*When everyone is calm.*
Today Jesus manages what everyone thought was impossible.

Jesus who died, is alive. Thanks be to God.

## Light the Gospel candle

*Give every child a candle.*

*Welcome the Gospel with a song*
Sing: 'One, two, three, four, five'. (See page 75)

*All stand (adapted from John 20:1-9)*

## Gospel

Mary Magdalene went to visit Jesus' tomb.
When she got there,
she saw that the large stone had been moved from the doorway.

She ran to tell Peter and John,
'Jesus isn't there'.
Peter and the other friends went to see for themselves.

When Peter got to the doorway he looked in.
He saw the clothes that Jesus had been wrapped in
lying on the floor.

Others looked too
and they believed.

Jesus is alive!

This is the Gospel of the Lord.
**Praise be to you Lord Jesus Christ.**

*All sit*

## Let's chat *Some suggestions*

Make an Easter candle or decorate your Gospel Candle to take home.
When you go back to church: Look at the flowers.
Listen for a word you haven't heard for weeks.
Does anyone know which word?...
It's... Alleluia.

The priest will say it twice at the very end of Mass.

Priest: Go in peace to love and
serve the Lord, Alleluia, Alleluia!

Us: **Thanks be to God Alleluia, Alleluia!**

# Surprise visitor

## Welcome

## Let's sing and say  (If celebrating the Introductory Rite, turn to page 74)

*Quietly by yourselves*
## Stop to think

Have you had any surprise visitors this holiday? Have you ever had a surprise visitor?
Who would you love to surprise you with a visit?

*When each child has had time to think*
## Share with each other

Do you like surprise visitors? Why?
Who do you like visiting? Why?
Do they ever bring you presents?
Do they ever ask you to do something for them?

## Light the Gospel candle

Today we hear how Jesus surprised his friends
with a visit. He brought a wonderful present.

*Welcome the Gospel with a song.  Sing Alleluia. (See page 75)*
*All stand*          *(adapted from John 20:19-23)*

### Gospel

Later on, on the same day
that the friends had
discovered the empty tomb,
they locked themselves in
because they thought the soldiers might
come looking for them.

During the evening Jesus came into the
room and said,
  "Peace be with you."

The friends were really pleased!

Jesus said again, "Peace be with you."
then he said,      •
  "As the Father sent me,
  so I am sending you.
  If you forgive people
  I will also forgive them."

This is the Gospel of the Lord.
**Praise be to you Lord Jesus Christ.**

*All sit*
## Let's chat  (some suggestions)

What did Jesus give to his friends?
How many times did he say "Peace be with you"? Why do you think he said it twice?

I suppose the friends could hardly believe their eyes and ears! Such a wonderful visitor and such a wonderful present.

Jesus wants us to pass on his peace by forgiving everyone, just like he did.
If we do this we will be very welcome visitors.

# Slow to believe

## Welcome

## Let's sing and say
*(If celebrating the Introductory Rite, turn to page 74)*

*Quietly by yourselves*

## Stop to think

Have you ever found something hard to understand and when someone has tried to explain you still don't get it or understand what they are saying?
Perhaps it's happened to you in school?
After a while it all seems clear and you really understand.

*When each child has had time to think*

## Share with one another

What is it like when you have to face new situations or understand new ideas / new ways?

What didn't you understand?
When did the 'penny drop'?  *(Explain the saying)*

## Light the Gospel candle

After Jesus had risen, he met two friends.
It was a while before the 'penny dropped', that they were talking to Jesus.

*Welcome the Gospel with a song.  Sing Alleluia. (See page 75)*

*All stand*                    (adapted from Luke 24:13-35)

### Gospel

On Easter Sunday morning, two of the followers of Jesus had to go to a place called Emmaus, and as they walked along, they talked about Jesus, about what he had said, and how he had died.

While they were talking, Jesus himself came and joined them, only they didn't see it was Jesus.

The stranger asked them both what they were talking about, and they replied,

"Don't you know about Jesus? We all thought he was going to be our King, but then he was killed three days ago. Now even his body has disappeared. Two of the women we know went to his grave and they told us it had disappeared! They said that Jesus was alive again!"

Then Jesus said, "You just don't seem to understand! Can't you see that he had to suffer and die like that. It was the only way he could win!" And he began to explain how the Bible had said that all these things would happen.

When they came to Emmaus, the two friends asked the stranger to stay for a meal, for it was getting dark. So Jesus went in with them, and when they sat down at the table he took the bread, he blessed it, and broke it into pieces and gave it to them to eat.

And all of a sudden they saw that it was Jesus himself!

They hurried back to Jerusalem to tell the other followers.

They said, "We knew it was him when he took the bread and broke it."

A. J. McCallen

This is the Gospel of the Lord. **Praise be to you Lord Jesus Christ.**

*All sit*

## Let's chat (some suggestions)

We all find Jesus, at times, hard to understand. It took the followers a long time – a whole day's journey.

For most of us it takes a whole lifetime to really understand and some people never understand.
Do you find Jesus hard to understand sometimes?
Do you find Jesus hard to believe?
What do you find difficult?

## Prayer

Jesus,
please help us to understand and believe
because we really want to.
Jesus hear us.
**Jesus please hear us.**

# Know his voice

## Welcome

## Let's sing and say (If celebrating the Introductory Rite, turn to page 74)

*Quietly by yourselves*

## Stop to think

What will your mum say if (or when) you take a picture home from church?
If you took it into school, what would your teacher say?

*When each child has had time to think*

## Share with one another

What would they say? If you begin to ask "Can I... (e.g. sharpen my pencil, play with...)
do you know what they will say before they say it?
When you don't know what to do and you're stuck, do you sometimes think "Well mum
would..., or she would say..."
We know mum well. We know what she would say and do in all sorts of situations. She
knows what is best for us.
We trust her.

## Light the Gospel candle

It's like that with Jesus, we know what he will say. As Jesus puts it, we know his voice.

*Welcome the Gospel with a song. Sing Alleluia. (See page 75)*

*All stand*      *(adapted from John 10:1-10)*

### Gospel

Jesus says,
The sheep follow the shepherd
to safety
because they know his voice.
They do not follow a stranger's voice.

The people listening didn't understand.
Jesus explained,
  "I am the shepherd,
  follow me and you will find true happiness.
  Don't listen to others."

This is the Gospel of the Lord.

**Praise be to you Lord Jesus Christ.**

*All sit*

### Let's chat *(Some suggestions)*

Why do you think Jesus had to explain?

Just like last week we sometimes have to think quite hard about what Jesus is saying to us. Jesus is asking us to put our trust in him, to follow him. This means thinking, 'what would Jesus say', whenever we have to make a choice. That's not easy, it means being kind to everyone, even people we don't like, it means sharing what we have and giving to others.

Shepherds protect their sheep.
Jesus will protect us.

# The Father and I are one

## Welcome

## Let's sing and say (If celebrating the Introductory Rite, turn to page 74)

*Quietly by yourselves*
## Stop to think

Who do people say you look like, mum, dad, uncle, auntie?
Who do people say that you 'take after', because you do the sort of things they would?

*When each child has had time to think*
## Share with one another

Who do you look like, take after?
When your mum and dad come to school the teacher often knows that they are your parents because they know you so well and they see the likeness.
Ask your teacher tomorrow if she can tell whose mum is whose by looking at the children in her class.
Adults often say, 'She's just like her mother!' What do they mean?

## Light the Gospel candle

This week Jesus tells us that we don't have to wonder what God the Father looks like or about what he would say or do. Now that we have seen Jesus the Son we know the Father because Jesus is just like his Father.

*Welcome the Gospel with a song. Sing Alleluia. (See page 75)*
*All stand* (adapted from John 14:1-12)

### Gospel

 Jesus said, "Don't worry trust me and trust God our Father. There is plenty of room in my Father's house, there is room for you all and I am going to get your place ready. Then I will come back for you."

Thomas and Philip didn't quite understand. They asked, "Where is this place, how do we get there?"

Then they said, "Show us the Father and we will be happy."

Jesus said, "If you know me you know my Father too. My Father and I are just like each other."

*All sit*

### Let's chat (some suggestions)

We don't need to look up in the sky wondering what God is like.
We have God to look at; Jesus!
Jesus is God.
What do you think about God?
Where is the place that Jesus is getting ready for us?
How do we get there?

This is the Gospel of the Lord.
**Praise be to you Lord Jesus Christ.**

# I will not leave you alone

*Welcome*

*Let's sing and say* *(If celebrating the Introductory Rite, turn to page 74)*

*Quietly by yourselves*

*Stop to think*

When you hear mum, dad and the other adults that you live with making plans to go out, is your first thought 'What's going to happen to me?' Do you keep asking? 'Are you leaving me on my own?' 'Who is going to mind me?' Sometimes it's mum, sometimes it's dad and sometimes someone else.

*When each child has had time to think*

*Share with one another*

Who do you like minding you?

If you could choose, who would you ask to look after you? Why?

When mum/dad is on the way out, do they say 'Be good while we are out' or 'Be a good girl/boy for me and I will bring you something'?

*Light the Gospel candle*

Jesus was getting ready to go back to his father. He promised to send someone just like him to be with us because he knew we didn't want to be left on our own.

*Welcome the Gospel with a song. Sing Alleluia. (See page 75)*

*All stand*         *(adapted from John 14:15-21)*

### Gospel

Jesus said to his friends,
    "if you love me,
you will be good and keep my commandments.
"I shall ask my Father
to send you someone to be with you
and to help you.
It will be just like having me with you.
I won't leave you on your own.

I will come back
and those who have kept my commandments
will be loved by my father and me.
And they shall see us."

This is the Gospel of the Lord.

**Praise be to you Lord Jesus Christ.**

*All sit*

*Let's chat* *(some suggestions)*

Are you good when the adults are out or do you get up to mischief?

When we are left on our own or with someone, it's because we can be trusted, to do what's right.

We all know what's right, it's up to us whether we do it or not.

Sometimes if we get up to mischief, we find ourselves in an argument or upset and we are glad to have mum and dad back to sort it out. If we don't get up to mischief then we can be quite happy till they return.

We should try to live happily till Jesus returns.

# I pray for them

## Welcome

## Let's sing and say

*(If celebrating the Introductory Rite, turn to page 74)*

*Quietly by yourselves*
## Stop to think

Do you pray? When do you pray?
Who do you pray for?

*When each child has had time to think*
## Share with one another

Who do you pray for? What do you pray for?
Why do you pray for... Though we should remember everyone, we often pray for the people who are very close to us.

## Light the Gospel candle

Jesus often prayed, he often prayed for us.

*Welcome the Gospel with a song. Sing Alleluia. (See page 75)*
*All stand*          *(adapted from John 17:1-11)*

### Gospel

Jesus looked up to heaven and said,
"Father the time has come
to let your glory be seen.

I have told the people you chose
all about you.
They know you sent me.

I pray for them.
They are close to us,
look after them.
I am coming to you."

This is the Gospel of the Lord.

**Praise be to you Lord Jesus Christ.**

*All sit*
### Let's chat *(some suggestions)*

Are you stuck when you say your prayers?
Are you not sure what to say?
The apostles weren't sure either.
Jesus told them to pray like this:
  Give glory to God, pray that we will live the way he has taught us, ask for things you need. Say sorry, and ask for help to be good.

Choose one of these ideas.
Quietly say your prayer.

**L O O K   A H E A D**
**Leaders: next week is Pentecost,**
**the Church's birthday.**
**Decide how you will celebrate.**
See page 97 'Let's Celebrate'.

# Believe Jesus is alive

## Welcome

## Let's sing and say
*(If celebrating the Introductory Rite, turn to page 74)*

*Quietly by yourselves*
## Stop to think

Have you ever tried telling someone
something and they wouldn't believe you?

*When each child has had time to think*
## Share with one another

Share stories about not being believed.

When? What was it about?
Did they laugh at you?
Did they walk away saying to each other 'take no notice, she's daft!', or shout 'Prove it!'
Did you keep trying to tell them or did you give up?
Can you make people believe?

## Light the Gospel candle

Jesus had appeared to his friends. They were very surprised to see that he was alive and
they were delighted! Thomas, one of the special friends, was out at the time, and when he
came back the friends were full of Jesus' visit. Thomas thought they were daft! A dead
man alive? He told them to prove it. Then Jesus appeared and stood in front of Thomas.

*Welcome the Gospel with a song. Sing Alleluia. (See page 75)*

*All stand*          *(adapted from John 20:29)*

## Gospel

 You know that I am alive
because you can see me.
May God bless all those people
who will not be able to see me
but will still believe in me.

A. J. McCallen

This is the Gospel of the Lord.
**Praise be to you Lord Jesus Christ.**

*All sit*

## Let's chat *(some suggestions)*

What do you think Thomas said or did next?

Who do you think Jesus meant when he said,
'Happy are those who have not seen and yet
believe'? Have you seen?
Do you believe? Jesus knew that people don't
always believe us.
They didn't all believe Jesus.

Tell Jesus all about it – he will believe you.

# Your sins are forgiven

## Welcome

## Let's sing and say
(If celebrating the Introductory Rite, turn to page 74)

*Quietly by yourselves*
## Stop to think

When do people say: "I can't believe my eyes!"
"It's too good to be true!"
"Well I never!" or "I'm seeing things!"

*When each child has had time to think*
## Share with one another

Have you ever said these things?
Have you ever thought it's too good to be true?
If you have, when? What was it about?

## Light the Gospel candle

This week we hear that Jesus appeared yet again to his friends.
They couldn't believe their eyes. In fact, they thought they were looking at a ghost.
That it could be Jesus, seemed just too good to be true. Then Jesus asked for something
to eat. They gave him some grilled fish and he ate it all up.

*Welcome the Gospel with a song. Sing Alleluia. (See page 75)*

*All stand*          (adapted from Luke 24:44-48)

### Gospel

It was written long ago
that I would die and rise again on
the third day
for everyone's sins to be forgiven.
You are my witnesses.

This is the Gospel of the Lord.

**Praise be to you Lord Jesus Christ.**

*All sit*
## Let's chat  (some suggestions)
What does Jesus mean by 'You are my
witnesses?'
What is a witness?
What does it mean for us?
How can we be witnesses?

Our sins are forgiven!
Is this too good to be true?
If you forgave someone would they think
it was too good to be true?

# Good shepherd

## Welcome

## Let's sing and say (If celebrating the Introductory Rite, turn to page 74)

*Quietly by yourselves*

## Stop to think

Who minds you when your mum or dad aren't around?
Big brother or big sister? Next door neighbour? Who?

*When each child has had time to think*

## Share with one another

Are brothers and sisters sometimes bossy? Do you complain about them saying 'You're not really in charge'? or do you say things like 'mum says..., dad says..., I'll tell them when they get home'.
Who do you like to mind you?
Can you hear your mum's footsteps coming down the street?
How do you know they are hers? Can she tell yours? Ask her.
The sound of footsteps are a special way of knowing each other.

## Light the Gospel candle

Jesus knows us each in a special way.

He is reminding us in this week's Gospel that he is a good minder and never bossy.
Jesus explained this to his friends, saying that he was like a shepherd who minded sheep (sheep need lots of care because they wander off and get lost).
He will take good care of us and never get us muddled or confused with each other.

*Welcome the Gospel with a song. Sing Alleluia. (See page 75)*
*All stand          (adapted from John 10:11-18)*

### Gospel

Stand and read the special words together:

"I am the Good Shepherd.
I know my own
and my own know me".

This is the Gospel of the Lord.
**Praise be to you Lord Jesus Christ.**

*All sit*

## Let's chat *(some suggestions)*

What do you think is special about you that Jesus loves so much?

# Stay close to me

## Welcome

## Let's sing and say

(If celebrating the Introductory Rite, turn to page 74)

*Quietly by yourselves*
## Stop to think

Stand up straight, stretch your arms out wide and wave your hands up and down.

*After a while when everyone has finished, sit down and wait until everyone is still.*

*When each child has had time to think*
## Share with one another

No one's arms fell off when you waved them up and down. Why not?
Where did the energy come from for your arms to move up and down?
*(Heart, body, inside etc.)*

If I cut off your arms would they be able to move up and down? Why?
They need to be attached to your body, otherwise they wouldn't have the energy to move.
What use can your arms and hands be when they move?

## Light the Gospel candle

*Welcome the Gospel with a song. Sing Alleluia. (See page 75)*
*All stand* *(adapted from John 15:1-8)*

### Gospel

Jesus said to his friends,
"Stay close to me!
and everyone will know
that you are my friends."

This is the Gospel of the Lord.

**Praise be to you Lord Jesus Christ.**

*All sit*
## Let's chat *(some suggestions)*

What could you do that would show you are a close friend of Jesus?
Perhaps you could think of something that has to do with your hands.
Draw your hand and write or draw your idea inside.
If you can't think of anything, think of Jesus. He will give you lots of good ideas.

You might try drawing some pictures of helpful hands and unhelpful hands.

# Love one another

*Welcome*

*Let's sing and say*
(If celebrating the Introductory Rite, turn to page 74)

*Quietly by yourselves*
*Stop to think*

How much do you love God?
This much... ?

*(Stand, place the palms of your hands together, then space them about 30cm/1ft. apart.)*

This much... ? *(60cm/2ft. apart)*

This much... ? *(arms stretched as wide apart as possible).*

*When each child has had time to think*
*Share with one another*

*Give the children time to stretch out their arms.*

God loves you more.

*Each of the leaders stand in front of the children in turn and let them see that your arms stretch further than theirs.*
*Then say* "God loves you this much more."

*Light the Gospel candle*

This week Jesus gives us a special rule to keep.

*Welcome the Gospel with a song. Sing Alleluia. (See page 75)*
*All stand* *(adapted from John 15:9-17)*

## Gospel

Jesus said to his friends,

"Love one another
as I have loved you".

This is the Gospel of the Lord.

**Praise be to you Lord Jesus Christ.**

*All sit*

*Let's chat* (some suggestions)

God loves us this much...
*(Leaders stretch your arms as wide as possible).*

Can you love people that much?
How can you love others?

# Jesus gets ready

*Welcome*

*Let's sing and say* *(If celebrating the Introductory Rite, turn to page 74)*

*Quietly by yourselves*
## Stop to think

When you say your prayers, what do you pray for?

*When each child has had time to think*
## Share with one another

What do you pray for? Why?
What do you say when you pray?
Where do you pray?
How do you pray?

## Light the Gospel candle

Last Thursday we remembered the day the disciples last saw Jesus.
Remember Jesus will come back again.

*Welcome the Gospel with a song.*
*Sing Alleluia. (See page 75)*

*All stand*　　　*(adapted from John 17:11-19)*

### Gospel

Father,
I love my friends very much,
keep them safe.
May they always be happy.

This is the Gospel of the Lord.

**Praise be to you Lord Jesus Christ.**

*All sit*

## Let's chat *(some suggestions)*

Who would you like to pray for?

Father I pray for .............................

Father I pray for .............................

Father I pray for .............................

Father I pray for .............................

Father I pray for .............................

**L O O K   A H E A D**
**Leaders: next week is Pentecost,
the Church's birthday.
Decide how you will celebrate.
See page 97 'Let's Celebrate'.**

# Peace be with you

*Welcome*

*Let's sing and say* (If celebrating the Introductory Rite, turn to page 74)

*Quietly by yourselves* Stop to think

Have you ever kept out of sight, hidden somewhere so that you can't be seen? Why did you hide? Where do you hide?

*When each child has had time to think*

Share with one another

When you were hiding, did you hide by yourself? Were you lonely or afraid? Did you hide with others? What did you say and do together? Did anyone discover you?

Light the Gospel candle

The friends of Jesus had hidden because they were afraid that the soldiers would come after them too. Jesus knew where they were hiding.

*Welcome the Gospel with a song. Sing Alleluia. (See page 75)*

*All stand* (adapted from John 20:19-23)

## Gospel

On the Sunday after Jesus had died,
Mary of Magdalene came to his followers and said "I have seen Jesus."
Then on the evening of the same day,
Jesus came and showed himself to them all.
It happened like this.

Some of the followers of Jesus were sitting together talking.
They had locked the door behind them because they were afraid
they might be arrested like Jesus.

But Jesus just came straight in and said "Hello."
"Peace be with you," he said,
and he showed them the wounds
on his hands and his side.
It was great to see him again.

Then Jesus said,
"My father has sent me to you.
Now I am sending you to help others.
I give you the Holy Spirit
to help you do this."
And he breathed on them.

"In future," he said,
"if you forgive people,
I will forgive them as well."

A. J. McCallen

This is the Gospel of the Lord. **Praise be to you Lord Jesus Christ.**

*All sit*

Let's chat (some suggestions)

Do you think Jesus gave them a surprise coming in like that? Perhaps that's why he said "Peace be with you". Were the friends pleased to see him? What do you think they might have said to him? Jesus gave them and us a very important message (read the last three lines of the Gospel again). What does this mean for us?
Who are we to forgive? If we forgive people they will never want to hide from us and they will always want to be our friends.

# Do you love me?

## Welcome

## Let's sing and say  (If celebrating the Introductory Rite, turn to page 74)

## Quietly by yourselves Stop to think

Have you ever said 'I love you' or do you think that's soppy.
Who have you said 'I love you' to? Perhaps mum or a friend.

Maybe you didn't say the words but you put
... 'love from' on a birthday card ... gave someone a really big grin
... gave someone a tickle or cuddle
Has anyone ever said, 'I love you' in anyway?

*When each child has had time to think*

## Share with one another

When do you usually tell each other 'I love you'. Sometimes when things go wrong?
Who do you love (mum, children's heroes etc)?
Would you do anything, anything for them to show them how much you love them?

## Light the Gospel candle

*Welcome the Gospel with a song. Sing Alleluia. (See page 75)*
*All stand* (adapted from John 21:1-19)

### Gospel

One evening Peter and his friends went fishing.
They stayed out all night.

In the morning they heard a man shouting to them from the shore.
"Have you caught anything?" They said "No." "Try again," said the man from the shore.

They threw their nets into the sea and caught so many fish they could hardly lift the nets.

Peter then recognised the man on the shore. It was Jesus.

He jumped into the water and swam to Jesus. The others followed in the boat.

They lit a fire and cooked some fish for breakfast.
After breakfast Jesus said to Peter, "Do you love me?" Peter said "yes."
Then Jesus said,
"Look after my friends, take care of them."
Jesus asked Peter this three times, which upset Peter.
Peter really did love Jesus and he didn't want Jesus to doubt it.

This is the Gospel of the Lord. **Praise be to you Lord Jesus Christ.**

## Let's chat  (some suggestions)

Why do you think Jesus asked Peter three times? How could Peter prove that he loved Jesus?
Explain the phrase 'actions speak louder than words'.
How can we show Jesus that we love him?

# You are mine

## Welcome

## Let's sing and say *(If celebrating the Introductory Rite, turn to page 74)*

*Quietly by yourselves*

## Stop to think

Without looking, how do you recognise your mum, (by her voice, footsteps)?
Without looking, how do you recognise your dad, (by his voice, footsteps)?
What about brothers and sisters?
How do you know them without looking?

*When each child has had time to think*

## Share with one another

*Let the children tell you all about their family*
*(but don't believe all they say).*

We know our family so well because they're ours.
We usually say  my mum     or our mum
                my dad      or our dad
                my sister   or our sister
                my brother  or our brother
We don't like to see anything nasty happen to them because they're our family.
It's the same for our friends. We take good care of each other.

## Light the Gospel candle

*Welcome the Gospel with a song.  Sing Alleluia. (See page 75)*
*All stand*          *(adapted from John 10:27-30)*

### Gospel

Jesus said
    "You are mine
I know each one of you
I will never forget you or lose you.
We will be together for ever.

God my Father
has asked me to take care of you
because you belong to us.

No one can ever take you away from us."

This is the Gospel of the Lord. **Praise be to you Lord Jesus Christ.**

*All sit*

## Let's chat *(some suggestions)*

Are you glad that you belong to Jesus? Why?
You still belong to your mum and dad.
They will always be your mum and dad
and God will always love you and take care of you.

Is there anything you would like Jesus to take care of for you? Pray quietly in your mind. Ask for his help.

*Pause*

Don't worry if you have forgotten someone or something. God knows you well, he knows all about your worries and he'll take care of them.

# Love one another as I have loved you

## Welcome

### Let's sing and say *(If celebrating the Introductory Rite, turn to page 74)*

*Quietly by yourselves*

### Stop to think

What's a copy cat?
When you play out do you ever play 'copycats'?
Think about the times you have been copied.

*When each child has had time to think*

### Share with one another

Do you like being copied? We all copy each other sometimes especially friends.
Who do you like to copy? What do you copy?

Copying each other, doing things together is sometimes a way of showing everyone that we are friends, that we belong together. Though sometimes being copied can get on your nerves.

### Light the Gospel candle

This week Jesus tells us that he wants us to copy him (it won't get on his nerves).
In fact he makes it a rule for us.

*Welcome the Gospel with a song. Sing Alleluia. (See page 75)*
*All stand       (adapted from John 13:33-35)*

### Gospel

One day Jesus said:
    Take care of each other.
This is my new rule:
    Love each other
    just as much as I have loved you.
    If you do, people will notice
    and they will say –
    "You are like Jesus".

A. J. McCallen

This is the Gospel of the Lord.
**Praise be to you Lord Jesus Christ.**

*All sit* ### Let's chat  *(some suggestions)*

What does this mean?
What do you have to do?
Think of ways that Jesus loved us...

*(encourage the children to be specific)*
he cared for the sick,
he never ran away from us,
he cared for the lonely,
he never hit anyone,
he loved the people everyone else hated,
he never said 'leave me alone' etc...
Could you copy just one thing this week.

### Prayer

Jesus please help me to copy you.

# I give you my peace

## Welcome

## Let's sing and say
*(If celebrating the Introductory Rite, turn to page 74)*

*(If celebrating the Introductory Rite, turn to page 74)*

*Quietly by yourselves*
## Stop to think

Have you ever been given a present?
Have you ever been given a present by
someone who was going away?

*When each child has had time to think*
## Share with one another

What sort of present were you given?
Why did they give you a present?
People often give us presents because they love us and it will help us to remember them.
Have you got any presents that remind you of someone?

## Light the Gospel candle

Today Jesus gives us a 'going away present'.

*Welcome the Gospel with a song. Sing Alleluia. (See page 75)*
*All stand*      *(adapted from John 14:27)*

*Welcome the Gospel with a song. Sing Alleluia. (See page 75)*

### Gospel

Jesus said to his friends,
"Don't be afraid,
I am going back to my Father.
I leave you a special present,
my present is Peace.

It's a present that only I can give."

This is the Gospel of the Lord.

**Praise be to you Lord Jesus Christ.**

*All sit*
### Let's chat *(some suggestions)*

Peace! What sort of present is that?
What is peace?

Whenever we are at peace or see other
people enjoying peace then we will remember
Jesus.

This week: If someone says to you,
'Just give me five minutes peace', then try
hard to do so.
It would be a lovely present.

# Be good friends together

*Welcome*

*Let's sing and say*  (If celebrating the Introductory Rite, turn to page 74)

*Quietly by yourselves*

## Stop to think

Has anyone ever tried to split you and your friend up, tried to stop you being friends?

*When each child has had time to think*

## Share with one another

How did someone you know break up a friendship?
Sometimes we can split ourselves from our
friends by an argument.
Being split up makes us very sad.
It happens to everyone at sometime,
*(be conscious of children from broken homes)* in some way.
Think of all the people you are close to. Who are they? Stay close to them.

## Light the Gospel candle

Jesus prays for us this week.
He wants us to stay close to each other.

*Welcome the Gospel with a song.  Sing Alleluia. (See page 75)*
*All stand*          *(adapted from John 17:20-26)*

### Gospel

Jesus looked up to heaven and said,

"Father,
I pray for all my friends
Keep them close to each other
as close to each other as you and me."

This is the Gospel of the Lord.
**Praise be to you Lord Jesus Christ.**

*All sit* **Let's chat**  *(some suggestions)*
How can we stay close to people?

### Prayer

For all the people we are close to.
Let's pray that we will always be close to them
Jesus hear us. **Jesus please hear us.**

For all the people that we aren't close to,
let's pray that we will become good friends.
Jesus hear us. **Jesus please hear us.**

For us here in the little church,
let's pray that we will always stay good friends.
Jesus hear us. **Jesus please hear us.**

> **L O O K   A H E A D**
> **Leaders: next week is Pentecost,**
> **the Church's birthday.**
> **Decide how you will celebrate.**
> **See page 97 'Let's Celebrate'.**

# The Holy Spirit comes to help

## Welcome

## Let's sing and say

*(If celebrating the Introductory Rite, turn to page 74)*

*Quietly by yourselves*
## Stop to think

Are you ever asked, at home or at school, to give a message to someone?

*When each child has had time to think*
## Share with one another

What kind of messages are you asked to give?
Do you like delivering messages? Why?
Sometimes we do, sometimes we don't, what makes the difference?

## Light the Gospel candle

This week Jesus wants us to send a message. It's a message we heard a few Sundays ago, so if you have forgotten, here's another chance.

*Welcome the Gospel.  Sing Alleluia. (See page 75)*
*All stand*            *(adapted from John 20:19-23)*

### Gospel

On the Sunday after Jesus had died,
he came back to see all his friends.
He said, "Peace be with you."
Then Jesus said,
  "My Father has sent me to you.
  Now I am sending you to help others.
  I give you the Holy Spirit to help you."
"In future," he said
"if you forgive people
I will forgive them as well."

A. J. McCallen

This is the Gospel of the Lord.

**Praise be to you Lord Jesus Christ.**

*All sit*

## Let's chat  *(some suggestions)*

What is the message? What have we to do?

Today we remember that the Holy Spirit is with us to help us. When the friends of Jesus began their message lots of people joined them and that's how the Church began. Today is the Church's birthday.
(This is why it's a special time to have a birthday).

## Let's celebrate

Sing: 'Happy Birthday to us.'

Blow up balloons. Make birthday cards.

# Know all about me

## Welcome

## Let's sing and say *(If celebrating the Introductory Rite, turn to page 74 or 102)*

*Quietly by yourselves*

## Stop to think

When you get birthday cards do they have different names on, such as:

| | |
|---|---|
| to my sister | to my friend |
| to my daughter | to my brother |
| to my niece | to my son |
| to my granddaughter | to my nephew |
| to my cousin | to my grandson |

Why do they have different names?

*When each child has had time to think*

## Share with one another

| | |
|---|---|
| Are you a daughter/son? | Are you a brother/sister? |
| Are you a niece/nephew? | Are you a grand son/granddaughter? |
| Are you a cousin? | Are you a friend? |

Now do I know all about you?

## Light the Gospel candle

Welcome the Gospel with a song. Sing Alleluia. (See page 75 or 104)

*All stand     (adapted from Matthew 28:16-20)*

### Gospel

Jesus said,
"Go tell everyone about me.
Help them to be my friends.
Baptise them in the...
name of the Father
and of the Son
and of the Holy Spirit."

This is the Gospel of the Lord.

**Praise be to you Lord Jesus Christ.**

*All sit*

## Let's chat *(some suggestions)*

Why do you think Jesus used all God's names?
(so they would know all about him)

Count the people to whom you are a
son/daughter,
sister/brother,
niece/nephew,
grandson/granddaughter,
cousin,
friend.

Are you two things to anyone e.g. sister and friend?

# I will return

## Welcome

## Let's sing and say   (If celebrating the Introductory Rite, turn to page 74 or 102)

*Quietly by yourselves*
## Stop to think

When someone is going on a long journey (sometimes even a short one), we often go with them to the bus, train, plane or car to wave.
Do you ever do this?
Who were you saying goodbye to?

*When each child has had time to think*
## Share with one another

Who was it? Where were they going?
How long were they going away for?
What did they say before they went?
What do they usually say before they go (if it's a regular occasion).

People's last words are important we want to make sure they get our message right. Sometimes they say 'I'll be in touch'.

## Light the Gospel candle

Jesus is saying farewell to his friends. He's going back to our Father but he will come back to us. It's not goodbye, it's till we meet again.

*Welcome the Gospel with a song.  Sing Alleluia. (See page 75 or 105)*
*All stand*          *(adapted from Luke 24:49)*

### Gospel

Jesus arranged to meet his friends on a mountain.
When they all arrived he said,

> "I want you to carry on my work.
> Go tell everyone that God loves them
> And to live good lives.
> Stay in the city until the Holy Spirit comes.
> Remember I will always be with you."

This was the last time they saw Jesus.

This is the Gospel of the Lord.
**Praise be to you Lord Jesus Christ.**

*All sit*
### Let's chat  (some suggestions)
What do you think the friends did next?

Do you think they missed Jesus?

Do you suppose they wondered how and when he would get in touch again?

FROM THE RISING OF THE SUN TO ITS SETTING PRAISED BE THE NAME OF THE LORD

# Ordinary Time

Moveable feasts and a three year cycle can make life very confusing! Easter is a moveable feast and consequently affects the order of the other Sundays of the year. Major feasts make a difference too.

The Church's year has the following usual pattern.

| | |
|---|---|
| Advent | is celebrated for four Sundays. |
| Christmas | is celebrated for two Sundays after 25th December. |
| **Ordinary Time** | starts with the celebration of the Baptism of the Lord and is followed by the 2nd Sunday of the Year, 3rd Sunday of the Year etc. There is a pause with the arrival of Lent which varies from year to year. |
| Lent | is celebrated for six Sundays, the final Sunday is Passion (Palm) Sunday. |
| Easter | is celebrated for seven Sundays and concludes with Pentecost followed by Trinity Sunday. |
| **Ordinary Time** | is resumed from the pause point before Lent. The Sundays of the year then continue in sequence until Advent, though they may be affected by major feasts. |

## Major feasts

When a major feast falls on a Saturday or Monday, then it is celebrated on the Sunday. The readings of the feast replace the Sunday readings. The feasts likely to be affected in this way are those fixed to a date:

| | |
|---|---|
| Mary Mother of God | 1st January |
| Epiphany | 6th January |
| SS Peter & Paul | 29th June |
| Assumption | 15th August |
| All Saints | 1st November |

The Ascension and Corpus Christi are fixed to Thursdays each year.

Ascension Thursday comes after the 6th Sunday of Easter.

Corpus Christi comes after Trinity Sunday.

If you are not sure, consult the Order of Divine Office and Mass for the Liturgical Year. It clearly states which Mass is to be celebrated. Your parish priest or parish office will have a copy.

# *Ordinary Time*
*From Baptism of the Lord (end of Christmas to Lent)*

## INTRODUCTORY RITE (1)

## Sign of the Cross

## Penitential Rite

Let us ask God to look on us
with love, understanding and mercy.
Lord have mercy.

*R. Lord have mercy.*
Christ have mercy.
*R. Christ have mercy.*
Lord have Mercy.
*R. Lord have mercy.*

*or sing:* Kyrie elesion

Jodi Page Clark

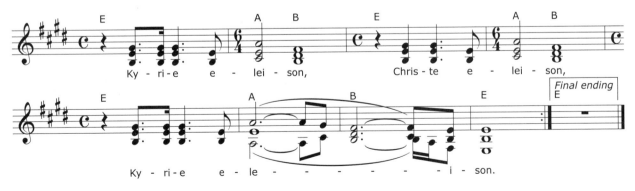

*Words & music © 1976*
*Celebration/Kingsway Thankyou Music*

# Gloria – Gloria, gloria in excelsis Deo (Clap, clap Gloria)

Mike Anderson

Glo - ri - a,— (clap)  glo - ri - a,— (clap)  in ex - cel - sis De - o.—

1 Lord God, hea - ven - ly King,—— peace you bring to us; we

wor - ship you,—— we give you thanks,— we sing our song— of praise.————

© Kevin Mayhew Ltd.

2 Jesus, Saviour of all, Lord God, Lamb of God
  you take away our sins, oh Lord, have mercy on us all

3 At the Father's right hand, Lord receive our prayer,
  for you alone are the Holy One, and you alone are Lord.

4 Glory Father and Son, glory Holy Spirit,
  to you we raise our hands up high, we glorify your name.

# Opening Prayer

*Let us pray*

Father,
Watch over us all
and keep us safe in your care.
Teach us how to live
so that we can all live
together happily.
We ask this as friends of Jesus,
Amen.

*End of Introductory Rite, turn to Sunday text* ➤

## Gospel Acclamation – Alleluia, hear the Lord

Traditional

(To the tune 'London Bridge is Falling down')

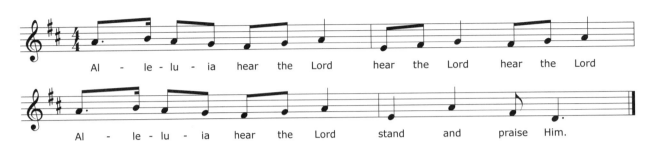

Alleluia    hear the Lord,
               hear the Lord,
               hear the Lord,
               hear the Lord.

Alleluia    hear the Lord,
               stand and praise him.

*Alternative:* – Alleluia

A. Gregory Murray

## INTRODUCTORY RITE (2) Ordinary Time *After Trinity into Advent*

## Sign of the Cross

## Penitential Rite

Lord Jesus,
you show us what is good
Lord have mercy,

Lord Jesus,
you show us how to love.
Christ have mercy.

Lord Jesus,
you are the Good Shepherd
leading us to everlasting life.
Lord have mercy.

## Gloria – Peruvian Gloria

Traditional

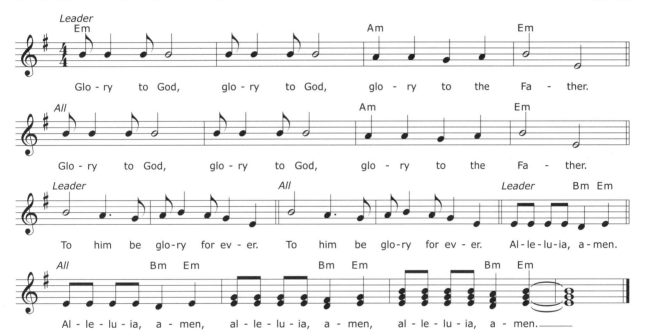

2  Glory to God, glory to God,
   Son of the Father. *(2)*
   To him be glory for ever, *(2)*
   Alleluia, amen. *(4)*

3  Glory to God, glory to God,
   glory to the Spirit. *(2)*
   To God be glory for ever, *(2)*
   Alleluia, amen. *(4)*

## Opening Prayer

*Let us pray*

Father,
We thank you for giving us Jesus
to tell us about your love.
May we become like him

so that everyone we meet
knows you love them too.
We ask this as friends of Jesus.
Amen.

*End of Introductory Rite, turn to Sunday text* ➤

## Gospel Acclamation – Alleluia, hear the Lord

Traditional
(To the tune 'London Bridge is Falling down')

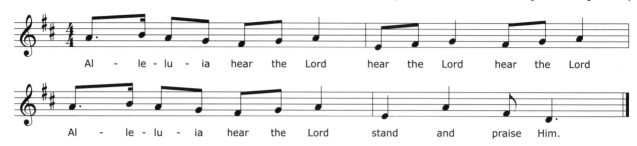

Alleluia    hear the Lord,
               hear the Lord,
               hear the Lord,
               hear the Lord.
Alleluia    hear the Lord,
               stand and praise him.

*Alternative:* Seek ye first the Kingdom of God

Karen Lafferty
*Words & music © 1972 Maranatha! Music*

2   Ask and it shall be given unto you,
     seek and ye shall find;
     knock and it shall be opened unto you;
     allelu, alleluia.

# Look, God's chosen one

## Welcome

## Let's sing and say
*(If celebrating the Introductory Rite 1, turn to page 102)*

*Quietly by yourselves*
## Stop to think

Have you ever had to be on the look out for a friend or relation?
Has mum ever said, 'whilst we're out, see if you can see... point them out to me'?
Perhaps you are the only one who can recognise them (your teacher, a friend's mum, cub/brownie leader etc.)

*When each child has had time to think*
## Share with one another

Have you ever recognised someone that no-one else new?
Sometimes we bump into people unexpectedly.
Have you ever been the first to see someone?
Do you get all excited and shout, 'look mum, there's...'? Mum stops and looks but doesn't know them and you have to explain who they are.

## Light the Gospel candle

This week we hear that John sees Jesus (whom he knows well) and he has to explain to other people who Jesus is.

*Welcome the Gospel. Sing Alleluia. (See page 104)*

*All stand*      *(adapted from John 1:29-34)*

### Gospel

Seeing Jesus come towards him
John said to everyone standing by
"Look, there's Jesus,
he has been chosen
to bring us closer to God."
John also said,
"It's been my job to point him out to you."

This is the Gospel of the Lord.
**Praise be to you Lord Jesus Christ.**

*All sit*
### Let's chat *(some suggestions)*

What do you think the people standing by did next?
Would they all believe John?
What would the people who didn't believe John do next?
What would the people who did believe John do next?
What would you do?
Do you believe John?
What are you going to do?

# Follow me

## Welcome

### Let's sing and say (If celebrating the Introductory Rite 1, turn to page 102)

*Quietly by yourselves*

## Stop to think

Can you think of anyone who is so wonderful that you would love to live with them? (And perhaps take mum and dad).

Perhaps someone who is on TV or someone in your street or someone in your school? Who? *(Give the children plenty of time to think)*

*When each child has had time to think*

## Share with one another

*(If the children give what they think is the wanted answer, i.e. God or Jesus or Mary, say yes and get them to think again).*

Who would you love to live with?

What's his/her name?

Who would you love to have live with you? Why do you think they are wonderful?

## Light the Gospel candle

Jesus met Peter and Andrew and they thought he was absolutely wonderful!

*Welcome the Gospel. Sing Alleluia. (See page 104)*

*All stand* *(adapted from Matthew 4:12-23)*

### Gospel

Jesus went to live in Capernaum, a town by the sea. One day he was walking by the sea and he met Peter and Andrew who were busy with their fishing nets.

They began talking and Peter and Andrew thought that Jesus was wonderful!

When Jesus said, 'Follow me, come help me in my work', they did, at once.

Then Jesus met James and John. James and John thought that Jesus was wonderful too, so they left their homes to be with Jesus.

They all travelled around the district together teaching people about God and making sick people better.

This is the Gospel of the Lord. **Praise be to you Lord Jesus Christ.**

*All sit*

### Let's chat (some suggestions)

What do you think about Peter, Andrew, James and John leaving their fishing nets and homes? Do you think it was hard or easy for them? Jesus wants us to join him in his work and we don't have to leave home. How can we follow Jesus?

# The way to real happiness

## Welcome

## Let's sing and say *(If celebrating the Introductory Rite 1, turn to page 102)*

*Quietly by yourselves*

## Stop to think

Have you still got all your Christmas toys? How many are broken?
Which ones do you still play with?

*When each child has had time to think*

## Share with one another

*(Let the children tell about their Christmas presents.)*

What new toy would you now like?
Toys don't last very long, they bring happiness for a while but we soon want something new.
Toys don't bring everlasting happiness.
For real everlasting happiness we will have to look for something other than toys.

## Light the Gospel candle

This week Jesus gives us a clue about how we can find everlasting happiness.

*Welcome the Gospel. Sing Alleluia. (See page 104)*
*All stand (adapted from Matthew 5:1-12)*

## Gospel

 One day Jesus went up a hill and lots of people came and sat down by him.

He said to them:

  Blessed are gentle people
  Blessed are people who forgive others
  Blessed are people who do what's right
  Blessed are people who think good
     thoughts about others
  Blessed are people who make peace and
     friends with each other

This is the Gospel of the Lord.
**Praise be to you Lord Jesus Christ.**

*All sit*

## Let's chat *(some suggestions)*

Jesus has said many things; which do you think is the most important? Why?
Do you know anyone who is gentle?
Do you know anyone who forgives others, forgives you?
Do you know anyone who does what's right?
Do you know anyone who says kind things?
Do you know anyone who is quick to make friends after an argument?
Are these people blessed, happy? Why?
Think again about what Jesus said.
Where is Jesus talking about you?

*(Leaders: the children will be reluctant to see the positive side in themselves, help them to do so.)*

Is it easy to be so blessed or is it hard work? Jesus is telling us that one day we shall be in the company of such people.
What will please you the most?

# Be at your best

## Welcome

## Let's sing and say
*(If celebrating the Introductory Rite 1, turn to page 102)*

*Quietly by yourselves*

## Stop to think

When people come to visit you or you go visiting, are you at your best?
When you are being at your best, what do you do?
What do you say?
What do you look like?

*When each child has had time to think*

## Share with one another

Tell us all about being at your best.
Do people like to see you at your best? Why?
Do you like people to see you at your worst? Why?

## Light the Gospel candle

This week Jesus is telling us 'always try to be at your best'.

*Welcome the Gospel. Sing Alleluia. (See page 104)*

*All stand (adapted from Matthew 6:13-16)*

### Gospel

Jesus says
You are some of the best people in the world,
but if you aren't at your best
what use are you to anyone?
No one hides their best things.
In the same way try always to show your best self.
People who see you at your best will thank God.

This is the Gospel of the Lord.

**Praise be to you Lord Jesus Christ.**

*All sit*

## Let's chat  *(some suggestions)*

Do you hide your best things?
Is it easy to be always at your best?

If everyone was always at their best the world would be a much happier place.
This is what Jesus wants.
This is why he tells us to be at our best.
He knows it's very hard and he still loves us even when we are at our worst.

Perhaps you would like to draw yourself at your best.

# Keep God's rules better than anyone else

## Welcome

## Let's sing and say (If celebrating the Introductory Rite 1, turn to page 102)

*Quietly by yourselves*
## Stop to think

Do you have rules in school? Don't run or don't go into a certain part of the yard? What rules do you have?

*When each child has had time to think*
## Share with one another

What are your school rules?

Why do you have them?

*(Help the children to see that they are there for everyone's good, e.g. 'Don't Run' is a rule to prevent us from bumping into each other and hurting each other. Help them to see the purpose behind the rule.)*

Are you keeping the rule if you don't run, only when prefects or teachers are looking? Are you keeping the rule if you never run? Is it possible to keep that rule even better?

## Light the Gospel candle

This week Jesus is telling us to keep God's rules at their best.

*Welcome the Gospel. Sing Alleluia. (See page 104)*
*All stand* (adapted from Matthew 5:17 -37)

### Gospel

Jesus said:
"Keep God's rules.
Put your whole heart into keeping them.
You know them,

Don't kill – but you must never even hurt someone.

Don't take what belongs to others – but you must never even be jealous of what others have."

This is the Gospel of the Lord.
**Praise be to you Lord Jesus Christ.**

*All sit*
### Let's chat (some suggestions)

What's the difference between just keeping the rules and putting your whole heart into keeping them?

Which way did Jesus keep the rules?
Would you like to copy him?
If you do people will think, isn't she/he just like Jesus.

Would you like that?

# Don't fight back

## Welcome

## Let's sing and say
*(If celebrating the Introductory Rite 1, turn to page 102)*

*Quietly by yourselves*
## Stop to think

Do you get much peace at home or do your brothers and sisters tease and torment you?
Do you get really angry inside and want to hit them?
What happens if you do – a fight?

*When each child has had time to think*
## Share with one another

Who blames who?
Do you say to mum 'He started it!'?
Does mum say 'You are as bad as each other!'?
Are you happy after a fight?

## Light the Gospel candle

This week Jesus is telling us don't be as bad as each other.

*Welcome the Gospel. Sing Alleluia. (See page 104)*
*All stand　　(adapted from Matthew 5:38-48)*

### Gospel

Jesus told his friends,
　"You have heard it said,
if someone hits you, hit them back.

'I tell you, if someone hits you, don't hit back.

'You know you must love each other.
Anyone can love their friends,
that's easy,
but you must love people who aren't your friends.

'If you do this you will be just like God.
God loves everyone."

This is the Gospel of the Lord.

**Praise be to you Lord Jesus Christ.**

*All sit*
## Let's chat  *(some suggestions)*

Is it easy to do what Jesus says?

Do you agree that people who fight back are just as bad as the people who started the fight?
Does anyone really win after a fight? What have they both lost?

Following Jesus is a really hard business! He knows this and even though we make a mess of it, he still loves us.

# Don't worry

*Welcome*

*Let's sing and say*    (If celebrating the Introductory Rite 1, turn to page 102)
(or Introductory Rite 2, page 105)

*Quietly by yourselves*

*Stop to think*

Is there anything worrying you at the moment?
Is there something that you feel you really need and perhaps you are worried that you might not get it or that what you will get you won't like.
What's on your mind? *(Give the children time).*

*When each child has had time to think*

*Share with one another*

*(If the children want to, let them share their worries. Take their concerns seriously, don't dismiss them whatever they are and allow privacy to any child who doesn't want to tell.)*
When we have a worry, it's 'on our mind' the whole time.
We keep thinking about it and we can't think about anything else.

*Light the Gospel candle*

Jesus knows we worry.
He knows that it takes up our time.
He tells us this week not to worry because God takes care of everything.

*Welcome the Gospel. Sing Alleluia. (See page 104 and 106)*
*All stand*    (adapted from Matthew 6:24-34)

### Gospel

Jesus said to his friends,
  "Don't worry,
don't worry about what you'll
have to eat,
what you are going to wear,
or anything like that,
there are other things to think about.

Look at the birds, look at the flowers,
aren't they beautiful?
God takes care of them.

You are much more important to him
so think how much more he will care for you,
and don't worry.

Don't waste time worrying about the future."

This is the Gospel of the Lord.
**Praise be to you Lord Jesus Christ.**

*All sit*

### Let's chat  *(some suggestions)*

Is it easy to stop worrying?
St. Augustine has some advice for us, he says: 'Leave yesterday to God's mercy, today to God's love and tomorrow to God's providence'.

*(Leaders: try and explain the meaning of this saying to the children).*

God will put right whatever we have done wrong, look after us today, and give us all that we need for tomorrow.

# Put into action

## Welcome

### Let's sing and say
(If celebrating the Introductory Rite 2, turn to page 105)

*Quietly by yourselves*
### Stop to think

Has your teacher ever given you a note to take home?
When she says 'be sure to give it to your mum and dad', do you say, 'Yes Miss'?
Then you run out of school and forget the note or you leave the note in your coat or bag for days. You said yes, you would give the note and you meant it, but you just didn't get around to doing it.

*When each child has had time to think*
### Share with one another

Have you ever been asked to give a note to your parents and not delivered it?
What happened because you didn't give the note? It's no good saying yes unless we really do get the job done.
*(Explain the saying, 'Actions speak louder than words'.)*

Perhaps you have made another kind of
promise and forgotten to keep it?
Do you think that it's important to keep promises? Why?

### Light the Gospel candle

Jesus knows that we are all quick to say yes.
This week he is reminding us that we have
to turn our words into action.

*Welcome the Gospel. Sing Alleluia. (See page 106)*

*All stand*          *(adapted from Matthew 7:21)*

### Gospel

 One day Jesus said
"Don't just come to me saying 'Yes Lord', you must really get on with what my Father wants."

This is the Gospel of the Lord.
**Praise be to you Lord Jesus Christ.**

*All sit*
### Let's chat *(some suggestions)*

It's very easy to say yes and mean it.
It is not so easy to actually do what we promise.

Put your words into action.

# Jesus chooses Matthew

## Welcome

### Let's sing and say *(If celebrating the Introductory Rite 2, turn to page 105)*

*Quietly by yourselves*

### Stop to think

Have you ever been picked or chosen for something special?
Perhaps you were invited to be a bridesmaid or you were given a special part in a school assembly or play.
Maybe you haven't been asked but there is something you would love to be invited to do.

*When each child has had time to think*

### Share with one another

What have you been chosen or picked for, invited to do? What would you love to do?
Have you ever thought 'I'm not good enough'?

### Light the Gospel candle

Today we hear about the time Jesus invited Matthew to be one of his followers.
Everyone was surprised because they didn't think Matthew was such a good person.
They didn't think Jesus should be making friends with such people.

*Welcome the Gospel. Sing Alleluia. (See page 106)*

*All stand (adapted from Matthew 9:9-13)*

### Gospel

 Jesus met Matthew while he was collecting taxes.
He invited Matthew to follow him.

Matthew was so pleased
he said yes right away.

Other people began to talk.
"What is Jesus doing,
why is he friendly with such people?
Matthew isn't a good man."

Jesus heard them and said,
"I haven't come to be with good people.
It's people who aren't good that need my help.
I have come to forgive them and help them."

*All sit*

### Let's chat *(some suggestions)*

Do you think Matthew was surprised to be chosen by Jesus as a friend?
Others thought he wasn't good enough, do you think Matthew thought so too?
How do you think Matthew would feel becoming a friend of Jesus?

Is anyone good all the time?
Jesus doesn't stop being our friend when we are bad.

What do you think about that?
Are you glad?

This is the Gospel of the Lord.
**Praise be to you Lord Jesus Christ.**

# Jesus gives his friends a job

## Welcome

## Let's sing and say *(If celebrating the Introductory Rite 2, turn to page 105)*

*Quietly by yourselves*

## Stop to think

How many friends have you? Count how many.
Have you ever needed their help?

*When each child has had time to think*

## Share with one another

What have your friends helped you with? We all need help from our friends, sometimes just one friend, sometimes lots of friends. There are times when only a special friend can help or someone who really knows us and understands us.

## Light the Gospel candle

There were lots of people who wanted help. Jesus felt sorry for them so he asked his twelve special friends to help.

*Welcome the Gospel.  Sing Alleluia. (See page 106)*

*All stand    (adapted from Matthew 9:36 – 10:8)*

### Gospel

There were so many people who needed help.
Jesus felt sorry for them
for there seemed to be no-one to help them.
He called his twelve special friends
and gave them the job.

Their names were:

| Peter, | Philip, | James (another), |
| Andrew, | Bartholomew, | Thaddaeus, |
| James, | Thomas, | Simon, |
| John, | Matthew, | and Judas |

Jesus told them to help as much as they could and to tell the people
that God's love is always very near.

This is the Gospel of the Lord.
**Praise be to you Lord Jesus Christ.**

*All sit*

## Let's chat *(some suggestions)*

Why do you think Jesus chose twelve?

*(It's really because of the twelve tribes of Israel but don't expect or give that answer. Allow the children their own imaginative response).*

We have a special name for the twelve; it's apostles. Nowadays we call the people who do the very same job bishops. Do you know any bishops? What is their work? Have you ever seen them at work?

Let's pray for our Bishop...

# Don't be afraid

## Welcome

## Let's sing and say  (If celebrating the Introductory Rite 2, turn to page 105)

*Quietly by yourselves*

## Stop to think

What do you know about yourself?
Do you know your height, weight and how many teeth you have?

*When each child has had time to think*

## Share with one another

How tall are you? How much do you weigh? *(Leaders excused!)*
How many teeth do you have? *(Leaders can include the false ones!)*
Do you know how many hairs are on your head? Exactly how many, not a guess, try counting. *(When the children realise it's impossible, move on.)*

## Light the Gospel candle

The twelve apostles weren't having an easy time. Jesus told them not to worry or be afraid.

*Welcome the Gospel. Sing Alleluia. (See page 106)*
*All stand        (adapted from Matthew 10:26-33)*

---

### Gospel

Jesus told the twelve,
"Don't be afraid!
Look around, there are lots of birds
and not one falls without God knowing
and you are more important to God
than them.
God even knows exactly how many
hairs grow on your head!
So don't be afraid.
God will take care of you."

This is the Gospel of the Lord.
**Praise be to you Lord Jesus Christ.**

---

*All sit*

## Let's chat  *(some suggestions)*

God knows even the number of hairs on your head! He knows more about you than even you know about yourself and he loves you.
You must be very lovable, perhaps more than you really know.
There is nothing to be afraid of, we are God's children.

## Let's sing

Rise and shine and give God the
glory, glory.
Rise and shine and give God the
glory, glory.
Rise and shine and give God the
glory, glory,
Children of the Lord.

Be brave and good for Jesus.
Do what's right although it's hard.

# Welcome

## Welcome

### Let's sing and say (If celebrating the Introductory Rite 2, turn to page 105)

*Quietly by yourselves*

### Stop to think

What makes you feel welcomed?
Is it a smile, a sweet or someone talking to you or is it something else?
What makes you feel unwelcome?
Is it being left at the front door, being ignored, told to get out of the way or is it something else?

*When each child has had time to think*

### Share with one another

What makes you feel welcome? What makes you feel unwelcome?
Have you ever been made to feel really welcome. Perhaps you have been invited to stay for tea or go out on a trip with your friend's family? How did they make you welcome?
Do you think it's important to make people feel welcome?
What difference does it make?

### Light the Gospel candle

Jesus wants us to make people welcome. He knows that it makes a difference.

*Welcome the Gospel. Sing Alleluia. (See page 106)*
*All stand      (adapted from Matthew 10:37-2)*

### Gospel

Jesus said,
"Put working for me first even though it's hard.

Make people welcome
and they will welcome you.

Even if you give just a cup of water you will be rewarded."

This is the Gospel of the Lord.
**Praise be to you Lord Jesus Christ.**

*All sit*

### Let's chat (some suggestions)

Is it easy to give a cup of water?

Jesus said put working for him first even though it's hard.
Could you make someone welcome by letting them ride your bike, play with your football or dolls?
Could you make them really welcome by letting them play with something quite precious to you?

This week: Try to share.
When your aunties, grandads or grans come to visit, rush to say hello or give them a kiss before your mum tells you, and don't go missing, spend some time with them.

# The children know

## Welcome

## Let's sing and say
(If celebrating the Introductory Rite 2, turn to page 105)

*Quietly by yourselves*
## Stop to think

Who is the cleverest person you know?
Why do you think they are so clever?

*When each child has had time to think*
## Share with one another

Who is it? What is so clever about them? Do you think you will ever be as clever?
Do you sometimes feel a bit stupid?
Does it sometimes seem that everyone else has the answer but you?

## Light the Gospel candle

Jesus tells us that it wasn't the clever people who first understood him.

*Welcome the Gospel. Sing Alleluia.* (See page 106)

*All stand*      (adapted from Matthew 11:25-30)

### Gospel

Jesus said,
     "Father, praise be to you,
it isn't the wise and clever people that
understand, it's the children!

We know each other so well
that I can tell them all about you."

Then Jesus said,
"Come to me I am gentle and kind."

This is the Gospel of the Lord.

**Praise be to you Lord Jesus Christ.**

*All sit*
## Let's chat  *(some suggestions)*

What did Jesus say?
What does this tell you about God?

Do you see how we come to know about
God? Do you like being with kind and gentle
people?
Do you know any?
Do you find it hard to be kind and gentle?

Perhaps you could try being kind and gentle
to just one person a day. You will soon get
into the habit. It will make many people
happy.

# Jesus tells us a story

## Welcome

### Let's sing and say  *(If celebrating the Introductory Rite 2, turn to page 105)*

*Quietly by yourselves*

### Stop to think

Do you like stories? Does your teacher or mum/dad ever tell you stories?
Sometimes they might tell a special kind of story, a story that will help you to understand something important. Have they ever told you about the 'Hare and the Tortoise'?

*When each child has had time to think*

### Share with one another

What is the story of 'The Hare and the Tortoise'? *(If the children don't know, tell the story.)*
What happened to the hare?
What happened to the tortoise? What is the special message in that story?
Does the story help you to think about the message, to understand?

### Light the Gospel candle

Jesus knows how much we love stories and how they help us to understand.
This week we hear one of Jesus' stories. See if you can understand the message.

*Welcome the Gospel. Sing Alleluia. (See page 106)*
*All stand         (adapted from Matthew 13:1-23)*

---

### Gospel

Jesus told this story,
    "Pretend that you are going out to plant seeds. Some fall on the floor and the birds eat them up.
Some fall on the edge of the path where the soil isn't deep, so the plants don't last long.
Others fall where there are lots of weeds and they don't last.
Some fall on lovely rich soil and they grow beautifully into hundreds of plants."

Some people went to Jesus to ask why he told stories. Jesus said,

"It's so you can understand.
You understand, the seeds are the ideas I teach you.

Some people don't bother to listen (my ideas are like seeds falling onto the floor, no good comes from them).

Some people try but give up because it's not easy.
(They are like the seeds on the edge of the path or among the weeds).

Some people listen and really try to make other people happy.
(They are like the seeds that fall on the rich soil – lots of good comes from them).'

---

This is the Gospel of the Lord. **Praise be to you Lord Jesus Christ.**

*All sit*

### Let's chat  *(some suggestions)*

Did you understand the message?
Did the story help you? Do you think Jesus was right to tell this story?
He tells lots more, listen out for them. Think again about the story, perhaps draw a picture.

# God is patience

## Welcome

*Let's sing and say* (If celebrating the Introductory Rite 2, turn to page 105)

*Quietly by yourselves*
## Stop to think

Have you a toy box or cupboard at home? Is it full of good toys and rubbish?
Perhaps little bits of things (Lego, toy-parts) might seem like rubbish to others, but they are precious to you.

*When each child has had time to think*
## Share with one another

Do you sometimes throw out the rubbish? What do you always keep? Why?
What's important, precious to you?
Are your precious things sometimes hidden under other unimportant things, so other toys sometimes get in the way of your precious ones?
When do you sort them out, rescue them?

## Light the Gospel candle

Jesus tells us another story this week. Listen for its message.

*Welcome the Gospel.  Sing Alleluia. (See page 106)*
*All stand        (adapted from Matthew 13:24-43)*

## Gospel

 Jesus told this story.

"Imagine a farmer planting seeds and while he is asleep along comes someone to spoil his field by planting weeds.

When the seeds start to grow the farmer notices all the weeds mixed up with the wheat.
The farmer's helpers offer to pull out all the weeds, but the farmer says,
'No, wait until they are fully grown then collect up the good wheat and burn the weeds'."

This is the Gospel of the Lord. **Praise be to you Lord Jesus Christ.**

*All sit*
## Let's chat  *(some suggestions)*

Anyone get the message?
Don't worry, the people listening didn't quite understand either, but Jesus explained.
Jesus will gather up all the good people to live with him and he won't miss a single person.
Inside each of us is good and a little bit of bad. Jesus wants us to try and change the bad parts. Throw them away, they are no use to you.
Keep tight hold of the good parts.

# *Precious things*

## *Welcome*

## *Let's sing and say*
*(If celebrating the Introductory Rite 2, turn to page 105)*

*Quietly by yourselves*
## *Stop to think*

What is your most treasured /precious possession?
Perhaps it's something that was given to you on a special occasion.
Perhaps it's special because it was given to you by someone special.
Perhaps it's very small and cost very little, but you think it's important.

*When each child has had time to think*
## *Share with one another*

What's your most treasured possession? Why? *(give each child a chance to speak)*
What would you do if you lost it? How would you try to find it?

## *Light the Gospel candle*

Jesus tells us that the Kingdom of Heaven is just about the most precious thing in our life.

*Welcome the Gospel. Sing Alleluia. (See page 106)*

*All stand* *(adapted from Matthew 13:4.4-52)*

### Gospel

Jesus said to his friends,
"The Kingdom of Heaven is like finding your most treasured possession.
You would swap everything you have for it.

The Kingdom of heaven is like finding something you have always wanted.
You would give up everything you have for it."

This is the Gospel of the Lord.

**Praise be to you Lord Jesus Christ.**

*All sit*

### Let's chat *(some suggestions)*

Think again about your own precious item. Would you swap it for anything?

*(Leaders: when the children eventually get to the point that they would not swap what they have for anything, then remind them that Jesus thinks they would swap it for the Kingdom.)*

Can you imagine the Kingdom of Heaven being that good?
Did you understand everything Jesus said? Have you any questions for him?

*(Leaders: Don't try to answer every question for Jesus. It is part and parcel of our life and faith that we have many unanswered questions. Leave the children with a sense of searching.)*

# Share – there is enough

## Welcome

## Let's sing and say

*(If celebrating the Introductory Rite 2, turn to page 105)*

*Quietly by yourselves*

## Stop to think

What's your favourite packed lunch?

*When each child has had time to think*

## Share with one another

What's your favourite packed lunch?
Have you ever shared some of it with someone else?
When did you share it and why?
Has anyone ever shared theirs with you? When and why did they do so?
Sometimes when we all share, we find that we have more than enough.
Do you ever take home part of your packed lunch?

## Light the Gospel candle

Today we hear how Jesus helped his friends to share their food.

*Welcome the Gospel. Sing Alleluia. (See page 106)*
*All stand*    *(adapted from Matthew 14:13-21)*

### Gospel

 One day Jesus and his friends were so busy
they hadn't stopped to eat
and the people who had been with them all day were hungry too.

The friends thought that Jesus
ought to send them home for their tea
but Jesus said, "Give them something to eat."

They told Jesus that all they had were
five loaves and two fish.

"Give them to me," said Jesus.

Then taking the food, he looked to heaven
said a blessing and gave the food out.

They all had enough to eat
and there was lots left over.

This is the Gospel of the Lord.
**Praise be to you Lord Jesus Christ.**

### Let's chat   (some suggestions)

*All sit*

If one of the friends had eaten all the loaves and fish, what would have happened?
If we are greedy (and keeping anything always to ourselves is being greedy) then other people go without.
I suppose you always watch that your brothers and sisters don't get more than you?
Who keeps guard in your house?
Have you ever noticed that you have sisters and brothers (we all have one Father – God!) in other countries who are dying because they have no food, is that fair?
Always try to do what you can to help, learn to share so that you will be able to share with Jesus.

# Trust Jesus

## Welcome

## Let's sing and say (If celebrating the Introductory Rite 2, turn to page 105)

*Quietly by yourselves*

## Stop to think

Have you ever tried learning to swim?  Have you ever tried learning to ride a bike?
Was it easy?  Were you a little frightened at first?

*When each child has had time to think*

## Share with one another

What is it like trying to ride a bike or swim for the first time?  Who helps you?  How?
You have to trust who is helping you a good deal.
Sometimes it's hard to trust and we panic, what happens next?

## Light the Gospel candle

Today we hear that the friends of Jesus had to learn to trust him, especially Peter.

*Welcome the Gospel.  Sing Alleluia. (See page 106)*
*All stand        (adapted from Matthew 14:22-33)*

### Gospel

Jesus sent his friends on ahead to the other side of the lake while Jesus stayed to pray.

During the night a storm came.
The friends of Jesus were in their boat sailing across the lake.
The boat began to toss and sway in the storm and the friends of Jesus were scared.

Suddenly they saw someone walking towards them, They couldn't believe their eyes.
"Is it a ghost?," they said.

But at once Jesus called out to them.

"Do not be afraid."

Peter said "if it's you Jesus, tell me to come to you."
"Come," said Jesus.

Peter climbed out of the boat and started walking towards Jesus across the water.
When he felt the wind, he became frightened and began to sink.
"Help me Jesus," he cried.
Straight away Jesus held out his hand.
Jesus said "Why didn't you trust me Peter?"

As they got back into the boat the wind dropped.
The friends in the boat all bowed to Jesus and said, "Truly, you are the son of God."

This is the Gospel of the Lord. **Praise be to you Lord Jesus Christ.**

*All sit*

## Let's chat *(some suggestions)*

At first the friends thought that Jesus was going to be a great leader, but bit-by-bit they were beginning to believe that he was the Son of God. Do you think what happened on the lake that night helped them?

Do you think Peter was brave? What would you have said, have done?
Jesus doesn't want us to try walking on water to show that we trust him.
He wants us to do as he says, be good to everyone. We show Jesus that we trust him in ordinary everyday ways!

# Jesus helps everyone

*Welcome*

*Let's sing and say* *(If celebrating the Introductory Rite 2, turn to page 105)*

*Quietly by yourselves*

## Stop to think

Have you ever been very busy doing something and someone has come along and interrupted you? Perhaps you were playing a game and you were sent for or perhaps you were painting a picture, watching TV?

*When each child has had time to think*

## Share with one another

When have you been interrupted?
Have you ever been interrupted when you were doing something that was really important, not just watching TV or playing?

## Light the Gospel candle

Today we hear about the day Jesus was interrupted.

*Welcome the Gospel. Sing Alleluia. (See page 106)*

*All stand*      *(adapted from Matthew 15:21-28)*

### Gospel

Jesus and his friends were walking along,
when a foreign woman started shouting,
"Help me, my daughter is suffering."

Jesus didn't answer and the woman kept on shouting.
The friends were embarrassed by her shouting and asked Jesus to help her.

Jesus said, "I was sent for our own people."
The woman came and knelt at Jesus' feet.
"I know," she said,
"but surely you can help me just a little."

Jesus said,
"You have great trust, your daughter is well."

And from that moment the daughter was better.

This is the Gospel of the Lord.
**Praise be to you Lord Jesus Christ.**

*All sit*

### Let's chat *(some suggestions)*

Jesus helps everyone! Why do you think he helped the woman?
How did the woman feel about Jesus?

There are shops which sell posters with sayings on them. Have you seen them? There is a special one about interruptions.

I couldn't get on with my work for all the interruptions.
Then I realised the interruptions are my work!

*(Leaders: try to explain the meaning to the children)*
Perhaps we can be ready to help everyone who asks this week.

# Who do you say that I am?

## Welcome

## Let's sing and say
(If celebrating the Introductory Rite 2, turn to page 105)

*Quietly by yourselves*

## Stop to think

Have you ever wondered about anything?
Wondered about how such a thing could
happen or where such a thing comes from?
Think about them for a moment.

*When each child has had time to think*

## Share with one another

*(Leaders allow the children a free response. Don't attempt to explain).*
What do you wonder about?
Do you know anyone else who wonders a bit too?
Have you ever wondered about Jesus?
What do you wonder about him?

## Light the Gospel candle

People had been watching and listening to Jesus for some time.
They were beginning to wonder about him.

*Welcome the Gospel. Sing Alleluia. (See page 106)*
*All stand (adapted from Matthew 16:13-20)*

---

### Gospel

 Jesus asked his friends this question,
"Who do people say that I am?"
They answered,
"Some say a wise man,
some say a great teacher,
some even say a good man from the past!"

Jesus asked his friends,

"Who do you say that I am?"

Peter answered,
"You are the Son of God."

Jesus replied,
"It's my Father who has helped you to know this.
Peter, I give you a job.
Lead my people, help them to find heaven!"

---

This is the Gospel of the Lord. **Praise be to you Lord Jesus Christ.**

*All sit*

## Let's chat *(some suggestions)*

Peter really knew Jesus!
Do you think that the other friends would agree with Peter?

Would everyone believe that Jesus was God's son?
What do you think the other people would still believe?
Does everyone in the world believe today?
Do you believe?

# No easy way out

## Welcome

### Let's sing and say *(If celebrating the Introductory Rite 2, turn to page 105)*

*Quietly by yourselves*

## Stop to think

Do you know any 'short cuts' from one place to another?
Do you know any easy ways of doing things?

*When each child has had time to think*

## Share with one another

What easy ways, short cuts have you found?
What would you love to find an easy way of doing?
What short cut would you like to find?
It's good to have short cuts, but sometimes it's not possible.
Is there anything that you have to do the hard way?

## Light the Gospel candle

This week we hear that Peter was looking for an easy way out of a situation.

*Welcome the Gospel. Sing Alleluia. (See page 106)*

*All stand* (adapted from Matthew 16:21-26)

### Gospel

Jesus began to explain to his friends that he would suffer, be put to death and rise again.

Peter was very upset at the thought of this and he said to Jesus, "This must not happen."

Jesus said,
"Peter that's not the right way."

Then he said to his friends,
"If you are to be a follower of mine,
you must not look for the easy way out,
you must be prepared to put up with
difficult times."

This is the Gospel of the Lord. **Praise be to you Lord Jesus Christ.**

*All sit*

## Let's chat *(some suggestions)*

Short cuts and easy ways are good and useful. But there isn't always a short cut or easy way; we sometimes have to do it the hard way. If we are followers of Jesus, then we mustn't avoid or run away from things because they are difficult.
Think quietly, what do you always run away from? Could you face up to it?

## Let's pray

Jesus,
you know the things I find hard to do,
please help me,
give me the courage I need.

Jesus hear us, **Jesus, please hear us.**

# Better together

## Welcome

## Let's sing and say *(If celebrating the Introductory Rite 2, turn to page 105)*

*Quietly by yourselves*

## Stop to think

Do you sometimes have to make an agreement with your friends or brothers or sisters?
Perhaps you have to agree together the rules of a game, what to buy for mum's birthday?
Perhaps you have to agree whose turn it is to turn off the light at night?
Perhaps something else, a TV programme, when you do your jobs?

*When each child has had time to think*

## Share with one another

What have you ever agreed to?
Is it easy to reach an agreement?
How do you manage it?
Do you expect the others to 'stick to it'?
What happens if they don't?

## Light the Gospel candle

Jesus is telling us this week that if we make an agreement together to ask for help in his work, God our Father will stick to it. He also tells us then whenever we meet together to do his work he will be with us, even if there are only two or three of us.

*Welcome the Gospel. Sing Alleluia. (See page 106)*
*All stand      (adapted from Matthew 18:15-20)*

## Gospel

 Jesus said,
"If you have an argument
try to reach an agreement
and keep trying.

I tell you seriously;
if two or three of you reach an agreement,
and if together you ask,
my Father will stick to it.

Where two or three meet together for me,
I shall be with you."

This is the Gospel of the Lord.

**Praise be to you Lord Jesus Christ.**

*All sit*

## Let's chat *(some suggestions)*

Whenever we meet to work for Jesus, to talk or think about him, he is with us.

What are we doing this morning?
How many of us are there (count)?
That's more than one, Jesus is with us as soon as we have more than one.

## Let's pray together

*God will hear our prayer.*
God our Father,
it's hard to agree.
Help us to know when we should say yes
and to know when we must say no.
Keep us together as good friends.

Father hear us, **Father, please hear us.**

# You have been forgiven
# – forgive others

*Welcome*

*Let's sing and say*
*(If celebrating the Introductory Rite 2, turn to page 105)*

*Quietly by yourselves*
## Stop to think

I want you to think about what might be a secret to you.
You must keep it a secret, you don't have to tell anyone.
Have you ever been in trouble; big, deep trouble?

*When each child has had time to think*
## Share with one another

Did you escape a telling-off or punishment
*(just a 'yes' or 'no')?*

If you didn't, do you wish you had?
How would you feel, or how did you feel, escaping the trouble?
We can be very relieved and thankful as it can put us in a good mood for a while.
We go about smiling and being kind.

## Light the Gospel candle
Today we hear about a man who was let off a great debt. Listen to how he behaves.

*Welcome the Gospel. Sing Alleluia. (See page 106)*

*All stand*    *(adapted from Matthew 18:21 -35)*

## Gospel

Peter asked Jesus, "How many times must I forgive someone, are seven times enough?"

"No," said Jesus,
"You must forgive seventy seven times."

Jesus then told Peter a story. *(Listen for the message)*

There once was a King who had lent a great deal of money.
He decided to send for all those who had borrowed from him.

There was one man who owed the King ten thousand pounds, and he couldn't pay a penny.
The King gave orders for everything the man had to be sold to pay off his debts.

The man pleaded with the King for more time.
The King felt sorry for him and let him go free, telling him to forget his debt.

On the way home the man met someone who owed him a pound.
He grabbed him by the throat and shook him.

"Pay me what you owe me," he said.
At this the man who owed the pound fell to the ground asking for mercy.
But the other man would not listen and had him arrested.

When news of this reached the King, he sent for the man.
"You wicked person, didn't I let you off your debt when you asked?
And yet you would not do the same for your friend!"

Then the King put the man in prison.

This is the Gospel of the Lord. **Praise be to you Lord Jesus Christ.**

*All sit*

## Let's chat *(some suggestions)*

What do you think about the man's behaviour?
Do you think it was fair for him to ask for his pound?

*(Leaders – it was fair, but Jesus takes us beyond justice to mercy. This is how he is with us and this is how we must be with others).*

No matter what you have done, no matter how bad you have been, God forgives you!
(His gift of forgiveness is free).
Because we have been forgiven so much we too should forgive others and not be like the man in the story.

# Jesus is generous

## Welcome

## Let's sing and say
*(If celebrating the Introductory Rite 2, turn to page 105)*

*Quietly by yourselves*
## Stop to think

When there is a cake for tea, do you watch carefully to see that you get your full share?
When anything is being given out, do you watch carefully to see that you have your share and that the others don't get more or better than you?

*When each child has had time to think*
## Share with one another

What sort of fair shares do you insist on? When there is a birthday in the house, does everyone get a present or just the person who is celebrating the birthday?
Is that fair? Are you happy that they are being made a fuss of?
Sometimes it's right that one person is treated specially, after a trip to the dentist, as a reward for hard work or as a thank you of some kind.
Does that sometimes happen?
When are you given the extra treat?

## Light the Gospel candle

Today we hear another story from Jesus.
Listen for its message.

*Welcome the Gospel. Sing Alleluia. (See page 106)*

*All stand*  *(adapted from Matthew 20:1-16)*

## Gospel

There once was a farmer who wanted to hire workers.

Each worker he employed agreed with the farmer that the pay would be one pound per day.

At dinner time the farmer met some people with no work.
He asked them to work and agreed to pay them.

At tea time he met some more people with no work, no one had offered them work all day so he asked them to work on his farm and agreed to pay them.

When the evening came he called the workers together and gave each of them one pound.

The workers who began earlier in the day complained, "it's not fair, we have worked longer than the others."

The farmer replied, "I am being fair,
didn't we agree that the wage would be one pound?
You have your money.
I will spend mine as I like.
Don't complain because I am generous."

This is the Gospel of the Lord.

**Praise be to you Lord Jesus Christ.**

*All sit*

## Let's chat *(some suggestions)*

*(Leaders – this is another story where Jesus moves beyond justice to mercy, generosity and real giving).*

Do you think it was fair? Why? The workers at the beginning of the day were lucky; they knew that they would have a pound, all day long. The others had this news much later.

What do you think the message is in this story? Jesus is generous and gives us all much more than we could ever earn. Be glad and say thank you.

# Yes, certainly

*Welcome*

*Let's sing and say*  (If celebrating the Introductory Rite 2, turn to page 105)

*Quietly by yourselves*
## Stop to think

Are you always being asked to do jobs?
Does it seem as though it's always you who is being asked?
What kind of jobs are you asked to do?

*When each child has had time to think*
## Share with one another

What jobs are you given?
Do you always do them as soon as you are asked?
Do you moan and then do them later?
Do you say yes, promise to do it later, and then forget?

## Light the Gospel candle

Listen carefully to the story Jesus tells us today. He has a question at the end.

*Welcome the Gospel.  Sing Alleluia. (See page 106)*
*All stand*       (adapted from Matthew 21:28-31)

---

### Gospel

There was a man who had two sons.
He went to one of the sons and said,
"Will you go and do a job for me today?"
But the lad said, "No, I won't!"
Then later on he felt sorry
and he went and did the job!

The Father went to the other boy
and said the same thing.

This boy said,
"Yes, certainly."
But he didn't go at all!
Then Jesus said,
 "Which boy did what his Father wanted?"

*(pause for responses)*

And everyone said the same,
"It was the first boy,
for he did the job in the end."

A. J. McCallen

---

This is the Gospel of the Lord. **Praise be to you Lord Jesus Christ.**

*All sit*

## Let's chat  *(some suggestions)*

Did you like that story?  What was the message?
Do you like Jesus' stories? Why? Do they have surprising endings?
There are lots more, we will hear another next week.

# Listen

## Welcome

## Let's sing and say (If celebrating the Introductory Rite 2, turn to page 105)

*Quietly by yourselves*

## Stop to think

Have you any toys that you haven't played with in a long time?
Has your mum ever said, 'Why don't you play with that toy anymore? If you don't want it I'll give it away.'

*When each child has had time to think*

## Share with one another

What's your reason for not playing with this toy for so long?
Has your mum ever given anything of yours away?
Sometimes it can be a bit like that with friends. If we don't bother to see them or play with them, they find someone else to play with. Is this true?

## Light the Gospel candle

The people aren't listening to Jesus so he tells them that his message will be given to people who will listen. He tells them in one of his stories. Can you hear his message?

*Welcome the Gospel. Sing Alleluia. (See page 106)*
*All stand     (adapted from Matthew 21:33-4.3)*

---

### Gospel

Jesus told this story,

"There once was a farmer who put some people in charge of his farm whilst he was away.

When the harvest was ready the farmer sent a messenger to collect it.

The people looking after the farm took no notice and chased the messenger away.

The farmer sent more messengers but the people still took no notice.

They chased them all away.

The farmer thought they will listen to my son, so he sent his son but they didn't listen to him either."

Jesus asked his listeners,
"What do you think the farmer will do when he arrives at the farm?"

*(pause for the children's responses)*

Jesus said,
"It will be given to people who will use it properly."

---

This is the Gospel of the Lord. **Praise be to you Lord Jesus Christ.**

*All sit*

## Let's chat  (some suggestions)

Jesus is telling us that we must listen to his message (Be good to everyone) and put it to good use or the message and the Kingdom of Heaven will be given to others.

Did you hear the message? Today say a kind word to everyone in your house.

# An invitation

## Welcome

## Let's sing and say   (If celebrating the Introductory Rite 2, turn to page 105)

*Quietly by yourselves*

## Stop to think

If your mum says that you can have a friend to tea, or to play or even a party,
do you love telling your friend? Is the best part of the party giving out the invitations?

*When each child has had time to think*

## Share with one another

Share stories of giving/receiving invitations.
Do you ever worry that your friend might not be able to come or might not want to come?
Has anyone ever let you down?
Have you ever wanted to go to a party that you weren't invited to?

## Light the Gospel candle

Jesus tells us another story.
It's about a wedding and the people who were invited.

*Welcome the Gospel. Sing Alleluia. (See page 106)*
*All stand*       (adapted from Matthew 22:1-14)

## Gospel

Jesus told this story,
   "The kingdom of heaven is like this:
A King gave a great party for his son's wedding.
Lots of people were invited.
But when the time came, they would not come to the wedding.

The King sent his servants.
'Tell them the party is ready.'

But the invited guests weren't interested.

The King was angry, he sent his servants into the town.
'Invite everyone you meet!'

All sorts of people came to the wedding, good and bad alike and the party was full!

When the King came in he noticed a man who hadn't prepared himself for a wedding, and he told his servants to tell the man to leave."

This is the Gospel of the Lord.  **Praise be to you Lord Jesus Christ.**

*All sit*

## Let's chat   (some suggestions)

Did you understand the message?
Is it very much like last week's message? *(Recall last week's)*
There is a place for us in heaven if we wish.

# A tricky question

## Welcome

## Let's sing and say (If celebrating the Introductory Rite 2, turn to page 105)

*Quietly by yourselves*

## Stop to think

Do you know any trick questions?
Here's one:
CONSTANTINOPLE is a very long word; can you spell it?

*When each child has had time to think*

## Share with one another

Can you answer the question?
The answer is 'It' Do you see the trick?
Do you know any other trick questions? *(Share trick questions)*
Trick questions are mostly asked for fun. We can all laugh at them.
Sometimes they are asked so that we can give the wrong answers and look stupid or get into trouble. They aren't fair questions.

## Light the Gospel candle

Some people who are not friends of Jesus tried to catch him out with a trick question. They wanted to get him into trouble with his answer.

*Welcome the Gospel. Sing Alleluia. (See page 106)*
*All stand    (adapted from Matthew 22:15-21)*

### Gospel

Some people came to Jesus and said,

"What should we do with our money?
Should we give it to the government or God?"

(They owed money to the government but they didn't want to pay.
If Jesus said God, they were going to blame him for their not paying up
and get him into trouble with the government.)

Jesus said,
  "Why are you trying to trick me?
  Give to the government what is theirs
  and give to God what is God's."

This is the Gospel of the Lord.
**Praise be to you Lord Jesus Christ.**

*All sit*

### Let's chat *(some suggestions)*

Do you think Jesus gave a good answer?
'Give to people what belongs to them'.
Does this make sense? Why do you think there were people who didn't like Jesus?
Perhaps they were jealous, perhaps they didn't like the attention Jesus was given.
Sometimes we do get jealous of other people and we try to get them into trouble.

Are you jealous of anyone?
Don't try to get them into trouble.

# Love God and each other

*Welcome*

*Let's sing and say*  *(If celebrating the Introductory Rite 2, turn to page 105)*

*Quietly by yourselves*

## Stop to think

*(Check whether they are about to have, or have had, half-term holidays.)*

What do you like to do during your half-term holidays? What is top of your list?

Do you like to celebrate 'Hallowe'en'?

What is top of your list that evening?

*When each child has had time to think*

## Share with one another

What is top of your list for half-term holidays?

Was it hard to choose one thing?

Are there so many things you would like to do?

What is top of your list for 'Hallowe'en'?

Can you give an answer that covers everything? When we
make a list, whatever we put at the top is the most important.
It might be hard to choose, we don't want to leave anything out.

## Light the Gospel candle

This week, we hear about when some people wanted to know which rule Jesus put at the
top of the list. They didn't really want to know. They wanted to trick Jesus.

*Welcome the Gospel.  Sing Alleluia. (See page 106)*

*All stand*       *(adapted from Matthew 22:34-40)*

**Gospel**

A group of clever people
went up to Jesus to ask him a
question.

They said,
"Which is the most important rule?"

Jesus replied,
"You must love God
with every bit of yourself,
and you must love others
as much as you love yourself."

All the rules are about this.

This is the Gospel of the Lord. **Praise be to you Lord Jesus Christ.**

*All sit*

## Let's chat  *(some suggestions)*

Jesus' answer covered everything! Do you think it was a good answer?

It certainly makes all the rules easier to remember. Now we only have to remember two.
Can you remember them? Could they go to the top of your list this holiday? How?

# Practise what you preach

## Welcome

## Let's sing and say

*(If celebrating the Introductory Rite 2, turn to page 105)*

*Quietly by yourselves*
## Stop to think

Do people often tell you to do something but they don't bother to do it themselves, *(e.g. don't cross the road in-between parked cars)*?

Do you have prefects in your school that keep telling you what the rules are, but don't bother to keep these rules themselves? Do they try to make themselves important?

*When each child has had time to think*
## Share with one another

*(Be ready for some embarrassing insights)*
What sort of things do people keep telling you to do?
We are all very good at saying what should be done and we are all very bad at doing what should be done.
Perhaps you don't 'practise what you preach'! *(Explain the saying)*

## Light the Gospel candle

Jesus reminds us that we must do what we say.

*Welcome the Gospel. Sing Alleluia. (See page 106)*

*All stand* *(adapted from Matthew 23:1 -12)*

### Gospel

Jesus said to the people,
    "Listen to what the leaders say and tell you to do
but don't copy what they do.

They do not practise what they preach.
They are only concerned with making themselves important.

You must not make yourselves important.
It's only God who is important.

You must serve and help each other."

This is the Gospel of the Lord.
**Praise be to you Lord Jesus Christ.**

*All sit*
### Let's chat *(some suggestions)*

When we are given a job, it's very easy to feel important and become bossy.
We sometimes see people doing this. We must not be like them.

Are you bossy sometimes?
Who are you bossy towards?
*(silent response)?*

Do you always do what you say ought to be done?

# Be ready

## Welcome

November is also a time for remembering people who have died.
Do you know anyone who has died?
Think about them for a while.

## Let's pray

God our Father,
we pray for our relations and friends who have died.
They are on their way to live with you now
and we know they will be *very* happy.
Help them on their journey.
Give them our love, we miss them
but we look forward to the day
when we shall be with them and you in heaven.
**Amen.**

## Let's sing and say *(If celebrating the Introductory Rite 2, turn to page 105)*

*Quietly by yourselves*
## Stop to think

Do you take a long time to get dressed or changed?
Is it because you can't find your socks or shoes or whatever, or is it because you get bored and begin to get interested in something else?

*When each child has had time to think*
## Share with one another

Why does it take you a long time to get dressed?
Have you ever not been ready in time?
Do mum and dad say 'We'll have to go without you'?

## Light the Gospel candle

Jesus knows that when we are getting ready we can be distracted, start to get interested in other things and not be ready on time. Listen to his story this week.

*Welcome the Gospel. Sing Alleluia. (See page 106)*

*All stand* (adapted from Matthew 25:1-13)

## Gospel

Jesus told this story,
"Ten bridesmaids got ready
and went to meet the bridegroom.
Five were foolish,
five were sensible.

The bridegroom was late
and the bridesmaids grew tired of waiting.

When the bridegroom came
the sensible bridesmaids were ready
and the foolish ones were not,
so the procession started without them."

This is the Gospel of the Lord.

**Praise be to you Lord Jesus Christ.**

*All sit*

## Let's chat *(some suggestions)*

If you were a bridesmaid would you be ready very, very early?
Perhaps you would be ready before anyone else! Why do you think the foolish ones were not ready?

We can all be ready on time to meet someone if we know when they are coming.
If we don't know when they are coming we can begin to get interested in other things and forget all about them.

Jesus will come again to see all his friends.

We don't know when, so we must always be ready, always at our best.
We could begin each day with 'This will be my best day', and finish the day with 'Sorry, I wanted this to be my best day', because it might not be.

Being ready for Jesus doesn't mean being perfect. It means trying to be good and saying sorry when we are not.

# Gifts

*Welcome*

*Let's sing and say* (If celebrating the Introductory Rite 2, turn to page 105)

*Quietly by yourselves*

*Stop to think*

What's your special talent/gift?
Have you a lovely smile, do you make people laugh or are you a good helper?
Perhaps you are good at games, a good reader, good dancer, good swimmer or good at riding a bike? Maybe you are always good to gran, good to the pets or good at being kind?

*When they have all had time to think of a special gift*

*Share with one another*

What's your gift? *(If the children don't name one, name theirs for them).*
What a lot of talent in this room!
Do you think that you could get any better at dancing, smiling etc?

*Light the Gospel candle*

Jesus has another story for us this week. It's about three people who were given talents.

*(Don't explain that the talents were money. If the children think they are gifts they will understand the spirit of the Gospel better).*

*Welcome the Gospel. Sing Alleluia. (See page 106)*
*All stand      (adapted from Matthew 25:14-30)*

## Gospel

Jesus told this story,
    "Three men were given talents.
The first was given five,
the second was given three,
and the third was given one.

Then they were left on their own to use the talents.

The first man worked hard at his talents and doubled them.

The second man also worked hard and he doubled his.
The third man kept his a secret and didn't use it at all.

When they met the one who had given them their talents,
they each told him what they had done.

He was pleased with the first man.
He was pleased with the second man.
He wasn't pleased with the third man."

This is the Gospel of the Lord. **Praise be to you Lord Jesus Christ.**

*All sit*

*Let's chat* *(some suggestions)*

Who do you think gave them their talents?
Who has given you yours?
When we give anyone anything, no matter how small, we love to see them use it.

We don't want them to give it away or put it into a drawer. We thought of it specially for them. God has thought of our talents specially for us.
He wants us to use them.
Do you think you could double yours? How?
*(Just by getting better at it)*

# Christ the King

## Welcome

This is the last Sunday of the Church's year. What will we have to wish each other next week? Does that seem daft?

## Let's sing and say (If celebrating the Introductory Rite 2, turn to page 105)

*Quietly by yourselves*

## Stop to think

Have you ever been kind to someone or done them a good turn?
Can you remember what you did, when you did it and why? Think hard.

*When each child has had time to think*

## Share with one another

When have you been kind?
(When everyone has had something to say)
What a lot of kindnesses! I'll never be able to remember them all.

## Light the Gospel candle

I can't remember all the kindnesses and perhaps you can't, but Jesus can and one day he is going to remind us all!

*Welcome the Gospel. Sing Alleluia. (See page 106)*
*All stand (adapted from Matthew 25:31-40)*

### Gospel

Jesus said,
"One day I will come back.
I will come to you and say,
When I was hungry you gave me food.
When I was thirsty you gave me a drink.
When I was a stranger you made me welcome.
When I had no clothes you gave me some.
When I was sick you came to see me.
When I was in prison you came to see me.
And you will be surprised because you won't remember, but I will.
Whenever you help anyone you help me."

This is the Gospel of the Lord.
**Praise be to you Lord Jesus Christ.**

*All sit*

## Let's chat (some suggestions)

Will Jesus have a lot to say to you?
Are you going to be kind this week?

How many more kindnesses will Jesus have to remember?
You don't have to keep count; Jesus will look after that, just get on with being kind.

# Come and see

## Welcome

## Let's sing and say  (If celebrating the Introductory Rite 1, turn to page 102)

*Quietly by yourselves*
### Stop to think

Why do you love to visit?  What do you do on these visits?
Who do you love visiting you?  What makes these visits special?

*When each child has had time to think*
### Share with one another

Dràw the children further.
'Have any of you a special place?
Do your brothers, sisters or friends follow you? Is it so that they can see it and join in the fun you have there?'

## Light the Gospel candle

Today we hear that John (the Baptist) and two friends were talking to each other when Jesus passed by. John said to his friends "Look, there's the Lamb of God." John's friends thought they would follow him to get a closer look. Jesus turned round and saw them.

*Welcome the Gospel.  Sing Alleluia. (See page 104)*
*All stand*              *(adapted from John 1:35-39)*

---

### Gospel

"What do you want?" said Jesus.

"Where do you live?" said the friends.

"COME AND SEE," replied Jesus.

---

This is the Gospel of the Lord.
**Praise be to you Lord Jesus Christ.**

*All sit*

## Let's chat  (some suggestions)

Where do you think Jesus lived?
What kind of house?
Who else might live there?
What did they do all day?
When would John's friends go home?
Why would they go home?

Perhaps you could draw a picture of Jesus' home with Jesus and his friends inside.

# Follow me

## Welcome

## Let's sing and say   (If celebrating the Introductory Rite 1, turn to page 102)

*Quietly by yourselves*

## Stop to think

Is there anyone in your house who is getting a new job?
Is there anyone who is thinking of changing their job?
What kind of job would you like?

*When each child has had time to think*

## Share with one another

Encourage the children to tell why the person is changing or getting a new job.
Ask the children if they have ever changed their minds about what they want to be when they grow up and ask 'Why'?

## Light the Gospel candle

Simon and Andrew were outside in the sun. They had just been fishing and they were sorting out their nets. Let's hear what happens next.

*Welcome the Gospel. Sing Alleluia. (See page 104)*

*All stand            (adapted from Mark 1:16-20)*

### Gospel

 Jesus saw Simon and Andrew and he said to them "Come with me, I have a special job for you."

Then Jesus saw James and John and he said the same to them.
They all left their jobs and followed Jesus.

This is the Gospel of the Lord.

**Praise be to you Lord Jesus Christ.**

*All sit*

### Let's chat   (some suggestions)

If you were there, what would you say to Jesus?
Did they know what Jesus was going to ask them to do?
Why do you think they said yes to Jesus?
What would they be thinking about as they followed him?
What was the special job?

This week try to do a job for Jesus.

# It's God who speaks

## Welcome

## Let's sing and say   *(If celebrating the Introductory Rite 1, turn to page 102)*

*Quietly by yourselves*

## Stop to think

Has your mum ever said to you, 'I don't know what's got into you today'?
What do you think she means?
How were you behaving?
What does your mum do and say?

*When each child has had time to think*

## Share with one another

When the children have shared their stories, ask if they have ever seen anyone in a 'twist with themselves'.
Why were they in a 'twist'? How did they behave?

## Light the Gospel candle

*Welcome the Gospel. Sing Alleluia. (See page 104)*
*All stand          (adapted from Mark 1:23-28)*

### Gospel

One day Jesus was teaching in a synagogue (church),
when a man came in shouting.
Something had got into him
and he was in a real twist with himself.
Jesus was sorry for the man.
The man asked Jesus for help
and Jesus said with a big smile:
   "Calm down, I'm here."

This is the Gospel of the Lord.
**Praise be to you Lord Jesus Christ.**

*All sit*

## Let's chat   *(some suggestions)*

Is it always easy to snap out of a tizzy?
When is it easy? When is it hard?
Perhaps Jesus can help us. We should pray to him.

# Let's pray

## Welcome

## Let's sing and say   *(If celebrating the Introductory Rite 1, turn to page 102)*

*Quietly by yourselves*

## Stop to think

Do you have a busy day?
What do you have to do each day?

*When each child has had time to think*

## Share with one another

Let the children draw or describe their day.

Do you sometimes forget things?
What do you forget?

## Light the Gospel candle

Listen to Jesus' busy day.

*Welcome the Gospel.  Sing Alleluia. (See page 104)*
*All stand*          *(adapted from Mark 1:29-30)*

### Gospel

After church, Jesus went with his friends James and John
to Simon's house.
When they got there,
they found out that Simon's wife's mum was sick.
Jesus went up to her bedroom to see her.
She quickly got better
and was able to make their dinner.
Then lots and lots of sick people came to Jesus.
He made them all better.
Jesus was tired out.
The next day he got up early by himself
to say his prayers.
Then his friends came looking for him.

This is the Gospel of the Lord.

**Praise be to you Lord Jesus Christ.**

*All sit*

## Let's chat   *(some suggestions)*

What must it have been like in Simon's house with all the people about?
Is your house sometimes very busy?

When you have a busy day do you forget your prayers?
When can you say your prayers?
Where can you say your prayers?
Who can you say your prayers with?

Write or say a prayer.

# Get well soon

### Welcome

### Let's sing and say
*(If celebrating the Introductory Rite 1, turn to page 102)*

*Quietly by yourselves*
### Stop to think

Do children sometimes run away from other children calling them names?
What sort of names do they call them?
How do you think they feel?

*When each child has had time to think*
### Share with one another

How does it make you feel when people run away from you?
How do you feel when they call you names?
Do children sometimes say, 'You're not allowed to play with us'?
What do they mean?

### Light the Gospel candle

In Jesus' time everyone ran away from lepers (lepers are very sick people and their sickness makes them look horrible).
Everyone had to keep away from the lepers in case they caught their sickness.
This was a special rule.

*(If the children interrupt with their own stories about measles or illness, let them share them with each other.)*

*Welcome the Gospel. Sing Alleluia. (See page 104)*
*All stand*         *(adapted from Mark 1:40-45)*

### Gospel

 One day a leper came to Jesus to ask for help.
Jesus felt very sorry for him,
so he touched him and made him better.
Then Jesus said
   "Don't tell anybody,
   just go home."

When the news spread, lots of people came to see Jesus.

This is the Gospel of the Lord.
**Praise be to you Lord Jesus Christ.**

*All sit*

### Let's chat  (some suggestions)

Why do you think Jesus said, "Don't tell anyone"? Are you glad that Jesus touched the leper? What would you have done if you had been there? Jesus gave that leper peace.

Let's say our prayer again:

   **Glory to God in the highest
   and peace to his people on earth.**

Draw Jesus making the leper better.

# Help our friends

## Welcome

## Let's sing and say (If celebrating the Introductory Rite 1, turn to page 102)

*Quietly by yourselves*

## Stop to think

Have you ever been stuck in a crowd and had to wriggle your way through?
Have all the people with you been able to wriggle through too?

*When each child has had time to think*

## Share with one another

*After a story or two, ask the children what would they do if they had been in a wheelchair?*
Think about your church.
How do people in wheelchairs get inside the church? What are the difficulties?

## Light the Gospel candle

*Welcome the Gospel. Sing Alleluia. (See page 104)*
*All stand* *(adapted from Mark 2:1-1 2)*

### Gospel

One day a crowd turned up at Jesus' house.
There were so many people that they could not fit in the house.

Along came some men with their friend on a stretcher
(he couldn't move his legs or arms so he had to be carried).
When they arrived at the house and saw the crowds
they knew that they would not get near Jesus.

They had a good idea.
They climbed onto the roof, made a hole
and let the man through the ceiling into the house.

Jesus saw him and made him better.
The man stood up, picked up his stretcher
and walked out.

Everyone was amazed.

This is the Gospel of the Lord.
**Praise be to you Lord Jesus Christ.**

*All sit*

## Let's chat *(some suggestions)*

When the man stood up he praised God. He shared God's goodness.
Can you show God's goodness standing on your own two feet?

Perhaps this week you won't push in the line at school and you will open doors and let others go first.

# Be happy now – Jesus is with us

## Welcome

## Let's sing and say    *(If celebrating the Introductory Rite 1, turn to page 102)*
*(or Introductory Rite 2, page 105)*

*Quietly by yourselves*

## Stop to think

Can you remember Christmas? What was it like in your house?
Did you put out all your best things? Were you at your best?

*When each child has had time to think*

## Share with one another

Why were we at our best? Did you try extra-hard to be good?
Did all the adults try extra-hard to be kind and patient?
Everyone put their worries to one side and said 'let's be happy, it's Christmas'.

## Light the Gospel candle

We have forgotten. We were so happy at Christmas because Jesus was born.
He is still with us so we can still be happy.
Before Christmas we ate ordinary food and did ordinary things keeping the best for
Christmas. In the Gospel we hear that some people in Jesus' time were still keeping their
best things for another day.

*Welcome the Gospel. Sing Alleluia. (See page 104 and 106)*

*All stand    (adapted from Mark 2:18-22)*

### Gospel

Jesus' friends were not fasting
and many people wondered why.
They asked Jesus' friends
"Why don't you fast?"
Jesus told them that the time to celebrate
and give thanks is now.
This was the time for doing
and being at your best.
The best that can happen has,
Jesus, God's Son is with us!

This is the Gospel of the Lord.

**Praise be to you Lord Jesus Christ.**

*All sit*

### Let's chat  *(some suggestions)*

Shall we make this week just like Christmas?
Give someone:    a smile,
                  a hug,
                  something to play with.

Tell someone:    a joke,
                  something nice about them,
                  something nice about
                  someone else.

### Let's Sing  *(four times)*

**Rejoice in the Lord always
and again I say rejoice.
Rejoice, rejoice,
and again I say rejoice.**

# Are holy days for doing good or bad?

## Welcome

## Let's sing and say

*(If celebrating the Introductory Rite 2, turn to page 105)*

*Quietly by yourselves*

## Stop to think

Sunday is like a holiday. What makes Sunday different from other days,

- everyone at home,
- everyone goes to Mass,
- no school,
- everyone lies in bed longer,
- everyone wears their best clothes?

*When each child has had time to think*

## Share with one another

Sunday is a holy day; it's the day that Jesus rose from the dead.
That is why we keep it holy. *How* do we keep it holy?

## Light the Gospel candle

Before Jesus died and rose again, the special day was Saturday.
The people of Jesus' time were very strict about not working or cooking on a Saturday.
People spent the day resting and saying prayers.

*Welcome the Gospel. Sing Alleluia. (See page 106)*
*All stand* *(adapted from Mark 3:1 -6)*

### Gospel

 One Saturday Jesus went to the synagogue (church).
A man with a sick hand came to Jesus for help.
The leaders were always telling Jesus and his friends off about doing helpful jobs on the Holy Day,
and they watched Jesus to see what he would do.
Jesus said,
   "Are holy days for doing good or bad?"

*(What do you think?)*

Jesus then made the man's hand better and the leaders were cross.

This is the Gospel of the Lord.
**Praise be to you Lord Jesus Christ.**

*All sit*

### Let's chat *(some suggestions)*

Are holy days for doing good or **bad**?
What do you think?
What shall we do?

How can we keep Sunday Holy?

# Be my family

## Welcome

## Let's sing and say
*(If celebrating the Introductory Rite 2, turn to page 105)*

*Quietly by yourselves*
## Stop to think

Who is in your family?
Who would you like to belong to your family?
Whose family would you like to belong to?

*When each child has had time to think*
## Share with one another

Share stories and family secrets!

What does it mean to belong to a family?
*(Leaders help the children to see the 'give and take' in family life)*

## Light the Gospel candle

This week Jesus invites us to meet his family.

*Welcome the Gospel. Sing Alleluia. (See page 106)*
*All stand* (adapted from Mark 3:31-35)

### Gospel

One day Jesus went home
and so many young people
came to see him
and he was so busy
that he didn't have time to eat anything.

When his family heard about this
they said he was mad
and they came along to help him.
But there were so many people outside the
   house
they couldn't get anywhere near him.
So they sent him a message, saying
Your mother and the rest of the family are
   outside
and they want to see you.

Inside the house
everyone was sitting round Jesus in a circle
and he looked round at them all and said
   "You will be my brothers and sisters
   and my mother as well,
   if you do what God wants you to do."

This is the Gospel of the Lord. **Praise be to you Lord Jesus Christ.**

*All sit*

## Let's chat *(some suggestions)*

Would you like to be a brother/sister of Jesus?
Perhaps you are already, how?
What does it mean to be a brother or sister of Jesus!

# God's power is in you

## Welcome

## Let's sing and say  *(If celebrating the Introductory Rite 2, turn to page 105)*

*Quietly by yourselves*

## Stop to think

What have you learnt this year?
What are you able to do now that you couldn't do last year? Are you surprised?

*When each child has had time to think.*

## Share with one another

Have you every heard the saying 'You don't know what you can do 'till you try it!'?
*(Explain to the children)*
This is what Jesus is saying to us this week.

## Light the Gospel candle

Jesus told a story about a farmer who planted some small seeds.
While he was asleep they began to grow. When the farmer saw them he was surprised to see the field full of plants. *(Do you remember planting seeds last Lent? Were you surprised that they grew so quickly?)*
The field looked wonderful.
Where did the power to grow come from?

*Welcome the Gospel.  Sing Alleluia. (See page 106)*
*All stand*                    *(adapted from Mark 4)*

## Gospel

Jesus says –
The Power of God is in YOU
to make the world wonderful.

This is the Gospel of the Lord.

**Praise be to you Lord Jesus Christ.**

*All sit*

## Let's chat  *(some suggestions)*

What would make the world wonderful?
What can you do to make the world wonderful?
The world is a big place.
It will be easier to start at home.

Jesus gave us a prayer to help us.
**Our Father...**

# Trust Jesus – do not be afraid

## Welcome

## Let's sing and say  (If celebrating the Introductory Rite 2, turn to page 105)

*Quietly by yourselves*

## Stop to think

Have you ever been frightened, really frightened?
What frightens you? Draw a picture.

*When each child has had time to think*

## Share with one another

What does or doesn't frighten you. Show your pictures.
Be brave, admit to what scares you, everyone is frightened of something.
*(Leaders tell the children what frightens you.)*

## Light the Gospel candle

*Welcome the Gospel. Sing Alleluia. (See page 106)*

*All stand*        *(adapted from Mark 4:35-41)*

### Gospel

One night Jesus said to his friends:
"Let's go over to the other side of the lake."

So they left the big crowds and got into a boat to go to the other side.
Then suddenly, the wind began to blow, and big waves splashed into the little boat so that it started to fill with water.

But Jesus was so tired, he just lay down with his head on a cushion and went to sleep.

His friends woke him up, and said,

"Look! we're sinking.
Why aren't you doing something to help?"

So Jesus sat up and he told the wind to stop making a noise, and he told the waves to stop rocking the boat.

Suddenly the wind just died away and the waves became calm again.
Then Jesus turned to his friends and said,
"Why are you so frightened?
You should know by now that I would not let you down."

A. J. McCallen

This is the Gospel of the Lord. **Praise be to you Lord Jesus Christ.**

*All sit*

## Let's chat  *(some suggestions)*

Think again. Look at your pictures and say together Jesus' words:
**I will not let you down.**
**Do not be afraid.**

Pray to Jesus whenever you get frightened.

# Jesus gives new life

*Welcome*

*Let's sing and say*
*(If celebrating the Introductory Rite 2, turn to page 105)*

*Quietly by yourselves*
*Stop to think*

Have you ever fallen or hurt yourself on a day trip?
Have you ever been sick and had to stay in bed
missing a good time?

*When each child has had time to think*
*Share with one another*

How did it happen? Who helped you? Did anyone send for help? Who was sorry for you?

*Light the Gospel candle*

In this story Jesus heals a little girl because her father goes to Jesus and asks him to
come and help.

*Welcome the Gospel. Sing Alleluia. (See page 106)*
*All stand (adapted from Mark 5:21 -24, 35-43)*

---

*Gospel*

One day a man called Jairus
came to Jesus and threw
himself down in front of him.
"My little girl is dying," he said.
'Come and hold her in your arms."
So Jesus went along with him.

Then someone came and said, "It's no use
bothering Jesus any more, your little girl
has just died."

But Jesus took no notice, and said to Jairus,
"Don't worry.
All you have to do is trust me."

When they got to Jairus' house, there were
lots of people there, and they were all
crying. So Jesus said,
"What's all this for?

The little girl isn't dead, she's only
asleep."

But no-one believed him. In fact, they even
laughed at him.

So Jesus sent everyone out of the house,
then he went into the room where the little
girl was lying and he took with him only her
mother and father, and Peter, James and
John.

Then he held the girl's hand and said,
"Get up, little girl!"
And she did and walked around the room!
Her father and mother were so surprised,
they just didn't know what to do,
so Jesus told them to give the girl
something to eat.

A. J. McCallen

---

This is the Gospel of the Lord.
**Praise be to you Lord Jesus Christ.**

*All sit*

## Let's chat *(some suggestions)*

What do you think she had to eat?
Who do you know who is sick?

## Let's pray

Lord Jesus,
please help ..................................... who is very sick.
Please help them to get better very soon
and help all the people who look after them.

# They didn't notice

## Welcome

### Let's sing and say (If celebrating the Introductory Rite 2, turn to page 105)

*Quietly by yourselves*

### Stop to think

Have your mum and dad been to school to see your work?
Were they surprised and amazed at how clever you have become?
Do you have to dance, sing recite poems for grans or aunties?
Are they amazed at how you can do so well, so young?

*When each child has had time to think*

### Share with one another

Share stories. What do people say? Do they say you take after your dad/mum?
Display one or two dances or songs.

### Light the Gospel candle

Welcome the Gospel. Sing Alleluia. (See page 106)
All stand             (adapted from Mark 6:1 -6)

### Gospel

One day Jesus and his friends
went back to Nazareth on a visit.
When he went to speak to everyone in the church
they were amazed at the clever things he said.
"Where did you get all this knowledge and learning from?"
Not everyone thought he was so good.
Jesus said
   "People who are with you all the time
   don't always notice."

This is the Gospel of the Lord.
**Praise be to you Lord Jesus Christ.**

*All sit*

### Let's chat *(some suggestions)*

Where did Jesus get his knowledge from?
Do people notice everything that is good about you?
Do you think you could notice something good about someone else?
Have a good look.

# Take his message

## Welcome

## Let's sing and say *(If celebrating the Introductory Rite 2, turn to page 105)*

*Quietly by yourselves*

## Stop to think

When you go out for the day, what do you take with you?
When you go on holiday, what do you take with you?
Make a list or draw pictures of what you take on a day out, a holiday.

*When each child has had time to think*

## Share with one another

Gather the pictures and pin them under the two headings. If there isn't time ask the children to call out all that they would take with them and write up their ideas on large sheets of paper. Don't accept general comments such as clothes, food etc. Encourage them to be specific and individual, ask: What kind? How much?

## Light the Gospel candle

One day Jesus called his friends together, put them in twos and sent them on a message (not a holiday).

What would be the message... ? To tell the people to be kind to anyone who is sad, to forgive anyone who hurt them, to give peace to anyone fighting, to be friends to the lonely.

*Welcome the Gospel. Sing Alleluia. (See page 106)*
*All stand (adapted from Mark 6:7-13)*

### Gospel

For this kind of message you don't need many things.

Jesus said:
"Take nothing for your journey,

no food,
no bags,
no money,
no extra clothes.

If people want your help give it,
if they don't,
leave them alone."

This is the Gospel of the Lord.
**Praise be to you Lord Jesus Christ.**

*All sit*

### Let's chat *(some suggestions)*

Do we really need all that's listed?
What really makes you happy – things? or no arguments? or friends?
Why did Jesus give them a partner?
Could you find a partner to take Jesus' message to someone this week?

Why not go back into church in twos and give everyone a big smile.
Don't take pictures or anything else.
Just a big smile.

# Jesus always has time for us

## Welcome

## Let's sing and say   *(If celebrating the Introductory Rite 2, turn to page 105)*

*Quietly by yourselves*

## Stop to think

Are you always being asked to do jobs in your house?
What kind of jobs?
Which ones do you like/hate?
Does it seem as though they only ever ask you?
Have you ever done two jobs one after the other and then someone asks you to do a third?
Do you say 'It's not fair.' 'It's not my turn.' 'I'm worn out.' 'Have I got to'!
'Our ............................. hasn't done any jobs.'
Or do you feel sorry for the person who is asking for help?
Do you say "O.K."

*When each child has had time to think*

## Share with one another

Share stories/experiences
*(Leaders tell the children when you've been 'too tired'; 'haven't had time'.)*

## Light the Gospel candle

After Jesus' friends finished their messages (refer back to last week) they came back to Jesus very tired. Jesus was very tired too.

*Welcome the Gospel. Sing Alleluia. (See page 106)*

*All stand        (adapted from Mark 6:30-34)*

### Gospel

Jesus said
   "You must come away for a while and have a rest."
So off they went in a boat for a holiday.
When they got off the boat,
crowds of people came to them.
They wanted to hear more from Jesus.
Jesus felt sorry for them.
He stayed talking to them
because they had no one to help them.

This is the Gospel of the Lord.
**Praise be to you Lord Jesus Christ.**

*All sit*

## Let's chat   *(some suggestions)*

Is it easy to help people when you are tired?
Do you think Jesus found it easy to be with the people when he wanted to be alone?
Where do you think the friends were while Jesus was talking?
Can you think of a job you could do without moaning this week?

## LOOK AHEAD

Leaders: Look ahead and decide if you will use next week's suggested activity.

# Enough for everyone

## Welcome

## Let's sing and say (If celebrating the Introductory Rite 2, turn to page 105)

*Quietly by yourselves*
## Stop to think

What's your favourite packed lunch?
Think of all the things you would love to have in a packed lunch.

*When each child has had time to think*
## Share with one another

*Share ideas.*
Make a list and draw pictures of all the items.
Try and persuade the children to 'give away their favourite item'.

## Light the Gospel candle

People had been listening to Jesus all day. They had had no dinner and it was past tea time, so they were really hungry. Jesus wanted to feed them but they moaned that they had no money to buy food for so many people.

Andrew noticed a little boy who had some of his packed lunch left. Andrew looked and thought, that's no use. The little boy had five bread rolls (with no butter, perhaps he didn't like butter) and two fish (perhaps he didn't like meat). The little boy gave his bread and fish to Andrew. Andrew gave the bread and fish to Jesus.

*Welcome the Gospel. Sing Alleluia. (See page 106)*
*All stand* (adapted from John 6:10-15)

### Gospel

Jesus said
    'Tell the people to sit down
on the grass'.
Then he took the food,
gave thanks and gave it out.
There was enough for everyone.

This is the Gospel of the Lord.

**Praise be to you Lord Jesus Christ.**

*All sit*
### Let's chat *(some suggestions)*

They had enough to eat because that little boy shared his packed lunch.
Sometimes we eat too much.
Does everyone in the world eat too much?
What would Jesus want us to do?
Let's put our words into action.

*Give out biscuits (to eat after Mass) to only half of the children. Pretend to run out and ask them what can be done about the situation. Hopefully, they will break the biscuits and share them with the children who haven't any.*
*or*
*Remind the children to pray at mealtimes, perhaps they could make up their own prayer.*

# Don't just think about food

## Welcome

## Let's sing and say  *(If celebrating the Introductory Rite 2, turn to page 105)*

*Quietly by yourselves*

## Stop to think

When you go out for the day do you like the picnic? Do you want it straight away?
After it's finished do you keep asking 'can I have some crisps?' can I have some ice
cream?' 'can I have some sweets?' Does your mum say 'food, food, food, is that all you
think about? Can't you enjoy yourself playing? Stop eating, there are other things to do.'

*When each child has had time to think*

## Share with one another

Share stories. If not all of the children have days out or holidays, encourage them to talk
about how often whilst they are playing they run into the house asking for things. Help the
children to see that there are other ways of enjoying themselves without lots of food or
money.

## Light the Gospel candle

Do you remember last week's Gospel? The boy and his packed lunch?
How Jesus fed lots of people?

*Welcome the Gospel.  Sing Alleluia. (See page 106)*
*All stand*           *(adapted from John 6:26-28)*

### Gospel

After Jesus had fed so many people,
they wanted to make him King.
They came looking for him but Jesus hid.
When they found him he said,
 "You are only looking for me for food.
 Don't spend your time just looking for food,
 you will soon have eaten it.
 It's better to spend time on things that last longer.
 I can show you other ways of living
 so that you won't think so much about food."

*All sit*

### Let's chat  *(some suggestions)*

What are the ways of being happy
during the school holidays?
Ways other than eating and spending
money?

Think of ways you can spend time
with your brothers, sisters and
friends.

This is the Gospel of the Lord.

**Praise be to you Lord Jesus Christ.**

# Bread of life

## Welcome

## Let's sing and say *(If celebrating the Introductory Rite 2, turn to page 105)*

*Quietly by yourselves*
## Stop to think

What's the most important food at a birthday party? The birthday cake?
What's the most important food on Pancake Tuesday? Pancakes?
What's the most important food on Easter Sunday? Easter eggs?
What's the most important food on Hallowe'en? Apples or chestnuts?
What's the most important food on Bonfire Night? At Christmas?

*When each child has had time to think*
## Share with one another

Share ideas. If there's time, draw pictures of all the important food.

*Welcome the Gospel. Sing Alleluia. (See page 106)*
*All stand* *(adapted from John 6:35)*

## Gospel

One day Jesus had to explain
how he was important for us.
He told us how he was even more important to us
than any ordinary food.
He was special food.
Jesus said,
"I am the Bread of Life."

This is the Gospel of the Lord. **Praise be to you Lord Jesus Christ.**

*All sit*

## Let's chat *(some suggestions)*

What does Jesus mean?

Has anyone made their First Communion? What was it like?

What does Communion taste like?

*(Encourage the children to talk about receiving the Blood as well as the Body of Christ).*

Is it ordinary bread? Wine? Who is it?

Why do you go to communion?

*(Children do not have to be good to go to Communion. They go to communion because they know they need Jesus' help to be good.)*

## Prayer

Jesus I want you to come and be with me in this special way.

I need your help at home, in school and at play.

It's not always easy to be good.

Grown-ups are often cross with me because I don't do the things they want.

Help me to know what is right.

Help me to be kind; to think well of others and to help where I can.

Dear Jesus, I love you.

I know you really are with me always.

Help me at work and at play.

Bless my family, my parish, my school and all my friends.

Sr. Margaret Bradley

# Living bread

## Welcome

## Let's sing and say
*(If celebrating the Introductory Rite 2, turn to page 105)*

## Stop to think

Do you eat bread every day?
Think about all the different ways you eat
bread (sandwiches, burgers, pizza, toast...).

*When each child has had time to think*

## Share with one another

How many ways do you eat bread and which is your favourite?
Sometimes we don't think about the bread in our food?
We are maybe more interested in the food that we are eating it with?

Bread is important food, without it we wouldn't have pizza, etc.
Bread is both ordinary food and special food, it also makes food special.

Jesus was a person just like us, ordinary and special.
He also made our lives special.
He came from heaven.
Jesus is living bread, he makes our lives special.

## Light the Gospel candle

*Welcome the Gospel. Sing Alleluia. (See page 106)*

*All stand*                *(adapted from John 6:51)*

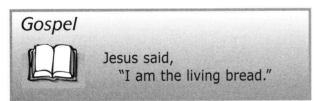

### Gospel

Jesus said,
"I am the living bread."

This is the Gospel of the Lord.

**Praise be to you Lord Jesus Christ.**

*All sit*

## Let's chat *(some suggestions)*

It's a bit of a riddle (we heard the same last week).
Jesus means that he is with us in our everyday moments.
Most of our everyday moments pass by and are forgotten,
but the moments with Jesus will never be forgotten by him.

When we go to communion we think about Jesus who is with us in a special way.

## Prayer

Jesus, I'm so glad you have come to be with me,
and to all these other people as well.

Thank you.
You know me.
You know the things I need;
the things I find hard to do at home,
in school and in the playground.

Please help me,
I am counting on your help
for you are brave and strong
I'm so glad you have come to be with me.

Sr. Margaret Bradley.

*Catechists: (Remind the children)*

Remember, we don't have to be good to go to communion.
We go because we want to become good.
We know that Jesus will help us.

# Jesus will never forget us

*Welcome*

*Let's sing and say* (If celebrating the Introductory Rite 2, turn to page 105)

*Quietly by yourselves*
## Stop to think
Can you do something that others can't ? Have a really good think.

*When each child has had time to think*
## Share with one another
What is it that other can do that you can't? *(Perhaps one or two could display their talents)*

When you tell the other people about it do they always believe you?
Do they say 'You must be joking', 'You're having me on' or 'Don't believe you?'
Has any one ever walked away saying 'It's not true' or 'Don't be stupid'?
It happened to Jesus!

*Welcome the Gospel. Sing Alleluia. (See page 106)*

*All stand*          (adapted from John 6:58-69)

## Gospel

Jesus said,
"Anyone who eats me and
drinks me,
I will be with in a special way
that lasts for ever."

Lots of people said "That's daft!"
and they walked away.
But Jesus' best friends didn't,
they said, "We believe you."

This is the Gospel of the Lord.

**Praise be to you Lord Jesus Christ.**

*All sit*

## Let's chat (some suggestions)
Do you believe in Jesus?
Can you eat and drink him? When?

Ask the children who do go to communion to tell the others what it tastes and smells like. *(Perhaps you could show the children altar breads and wine, and invite them to taste. Explain how it is not yet ready to be Jesus).*

Are any of you getting ready to make your First Communion?
*(All children, whatever their age are in some way preparing for Communion).*

Can't you wait?

Jesus can't wait either! Perhaps at communion time you can go to the altar and Father will give you a blessing to let you know that Jesus is with you in a different, special way. *(Check with the priest first.)*

Will you believe him?

# The important things

## Welcome

## Let's sing and say *(If celebrating the Introductory Rite 2, turn to page 105)*

*Quietly by yourselves*

## Stop to think

Do you know anyone who makes a fuss about getting ready for school?
They want new pencils, new bag, new uniform...

*When each child has had time to think*

## Share with one another

Do all these things make such a difference in school?
Does your mum sometimes say 'Stop making a fuss and get off to school' or 'Don't worry about these things, just do your best'?
Does your school teacher sometimes say, 'Stop making a fuss, sit down and get on with your work. That's what you have to get on with, stop worrying'?

## Light the Gospel candle

There was a rule in Jesus' time. People had to wash before they ate.
Some people made a great fuss and had a shower or a bath.
Jesus and his friends didn't always wash as much. The leaders asked Jesus 'Why?'.

*Welcome the Gospel. Sing Alleluia. (See page 106)*
*All stand (adapted from Mark 7:21 -23)*

## Gospel

Jesus said,
   "Washing your hands and having baths doesn't make you good.
It's what you say, do and think, that matters.
It's what goes on inside you,
not outside you,
that counts."

This is the Gospel of the Lord.
**Praise be to you Lord Jesus Christ.**

*All sit*

## Let's chat *(some suggestions)*

Write (or draw) the good things inside you.
Draw two pictures: Me at my best outside and Me at my best inside.

# Hear the Lord

*Welcome*

*Let's sing and say* (If celebrating the Introductory Rite 2, turn to page 105)

*Quietly by yourselves*

## Stop to think

Close your eyes, sit very still and listen.

*When each child has had time to think*

## Share with one another

What did you hear? What would it be like if you couldn't hear at all? Do you know anyone who is deaf? If you were deaf what sounds would you miss most?

*Welcome the Gospel. Sing Alleluia. (See page 106)*
*All stand*      (adapted from Mark 7:31-37)

---

### Gospel

One day Jesus was on his way to the Sea of Galilee when some people brought a deaf man to him.
Jesus felt sorry for him.
He put his hands on his ears and on his mouth
and the man could hear!
Everyone was very pleased.

---

This is the Gospel of the Lord.
**Praise be to you Lord Jesus Christ.**

*All sit*

## Let's chat *(some suggestions)*

What do you think the man's favourite sound would be?
What's your favourite sound?
What words do you love to hear?
How could you speak to a deaf person?

# Jesus is God's Son

## Welcome

## Let's sing and say *(If celebrating the Introductory Rite 2, turn to page 105)*

*Quietly by yourselves*

## Stop to think

Which class are you in?
Are you sometimes called Miss ..........................'s   class

or    Middle Infants,
Tops,
First-year Juniors, etc.

Do people sometimes ask you which class you are in?

*When each child has had time to think*

## Share with one another

Whose class do you say you are in?
What's different about being in top infants/First year Juniors/Second year Juniors etc.?
Are there more jobs?
What does Miss ask of you now that you are ................................. ?

## Light the Gospel candle

One day when Jesus was walking along the road with his friends, he asked them a question.

*Welcome the Gospel.  Sing Alleluia. (See page 106)*

*All stand    (adapted from Mark 8:27-30, 34-35)*

---

### Gospel

Jesus said,
"Who do people say that I am?"

Peter said, "You are God's Son."

Jesus told his friends
that being his friend
means putting up with difficult times.

---

This is the Gospel of the Lord.

**Praise be to you Lord Jesus Christ.**

*All sit*

## Let's chat  *(some suggestions)*

What are your difficult times?
What do you have to put up with?

# Put yourself last

## Welcome

## Let's sing and say

*(If celebrating the Introductory Rite 2, turn to page 105)*

*Quietly by yourselves*

## Stop to think

Do you know people who keep putting themselves 'in charge'? Have you been put in charge of anything? Do you sometimes put yourself in charge?

*When each child has had time to think*

## Share with one another

*(Encourage the children to be conscious of the times they have perhaps been bossy. Put themselves at the front of the class line in the yard, etc. Wanted to be 'top dog'.)*

Was there ever a time when you thought you were the best at something and someone else surprised you by doing it better?

## Light the Gospel candle

One day Jesus and his friends were going to the town of Capernaum.
The friends started to make a fuss.
Jesus asked them "What are you arguing about?"
They were too ashamed to answer.
They had been arguing about who should be the leader.

*Welcome the Gospel. Sing Alleluia. (See page 106)*

*All stand (adapted from Mark 9:35-37)*

| Gospel |
| --- |
| Jesus said, "If anyone wants to be first, he must make himself last of all and be the servant of all." |

This is the Gospel of the Lord.

**Praise be to you Lord Jesus Christ.**

*All sit*

## Let's chat *(some suggestions)*

What did Jesus mean?
What does being a servant mean?
Do you know any servants?
Who are the people who serve you?
Who would you like to serve?

# God's work is done by all sorts of people

## Welcome

## Let's sing and say *(If celebrating the Introductory Rite 2, turn to page 105)*

*Quietly by yourselves*

## Stop to think

Do you know anyone who doesn't go to Church?
Are they good people?  Do they do good things?

*When each child has had time to think*

## Share with one another

Encourage the children to name all the goodness in their non-Catholic friends and family.
Encourage the children to see and name the goodness in their Catholic friends and family who might not go to Mass.
Help them to see that in many ways they know and love Jesus too.

## Light the Gospel candle

One day John (Jesus' friend) came to Jesus in a worried state. A man who was not a follower of Jesus had been copying him, doing what Jesus and his friends did.
This man told people that Jesus said he could do these things for him.
John had tried to stop him.

*Welcome the Gospel. Sing Alleluia. (See page 106)*
*All stand*                    *(adapted from Mark 9:45)*

 **Gospel**

Jesus said,
"You must not stop him
if he is doing good."

This is the Gospel of the Lord.
**Praise be to you Lord Jesus Christ.**

*All sit*

## Let's chat  *(some suggestions)*

Did you think the man was doing good?

Draw a picture of all the good people you know doing good things because they love Jesus too.

Thank you Jesus for all these good people.

# Let the children come

*Welcome*

*Let's sing and say*
(If celebrating the Introductory Rite 2, turn to page 105)

*Quietly by yourselves*

*Stop to think*

Where aren't children allowed?
Have you ever been left out, told that you
are too young to join in?

*When each child has had time to think*

*Share with one another*

When did it happen to you?
Why do you think adults don't always want
children around?
Sometimes because it's dangerous.
Sometimes it's because it's late and children need their sleep.
Sometimes it's because children run about and get under everyone's feet.

*Light the Gospel candle*

One day mums and dads brought their children to meet Jesus.
They wanted Jesus to bless them.
The friends of Jesus (the apostles) tried to send them away.

*Welcome the Gospel. Sing Alleluia. (See page 106)*
*All stand (adapted from Mark 10:13-16)*

 **Gospel**

Jesus saw what was happening
and he said,

"Never send the children away,
let them come to me".

Then he put his arms around them
and gave them his blessing.

This is the Gospel of the Lord.
**Praise be to you Lord Jesus Christ.**

*All sit*

*Let's chat* (some suggestions)

Jesus never turns anyone away.
What would you have done if you had been there?
Would you be too scared to go forward?
Would you only go forward if your sister/brother went with you?
Would you have jumped onto his knee, touched his beard?
Do you like the feel of beards?
Where would you have stood?
What would you have said to Jesus?
What do you think he would have said to you?

# Don't just keep the rules

## Welcome

## Let's sing and say (If celebrating the Introductory Rite 2, turn to page 105)

*Quietly by yourselves*
## Stop to think

Do you have any rules at home?
Do you have any rules at school? Are they easy to keep?

*When each child has had time to think*
## Share with one another

What are the rules? Do you keep them?
Why do you think we have rules?  Yes, they're for everyone's good, they make things fair.

## Light the Gospel candle

One day a young man came up to Jesus.
He said, "Sir, what must I do to get to heaven?"
Jesus asked him if he kept all the rules. "Yes, ever since I was very small,"
said the young man.

*Welcome the Gospel. Sing Alleluia. (See page 106)*
*All stand (adapted from Mark 10:21-22)*

### Gospel

Jesus looked at him and smiled because he loved him.
Jesus said,
"Go and sell everything you have and give all your money to the poor."
This was too hard for the young man to do and he went home feeling sad.

This is the Gospel of the Lord.

**Praise be to you Lord Jesus Christ.**

*All sit*

## Let's chat *(some suggestions)*

Do you think the man will go to heaven?
He probably will. Jesus loved him, even if he could not do the extra thing Jesus asked.

Is it easy to give away money?
Have you ever given away money?
Why did Jesus ask the young man to do this?
Draw your money box.
Would you like to give some of your money to the poor?

# It can be a hard life

## Welcome

## Let's sing and say
*(If celebrating the Introductory Rite 2, turn to page 105)*

*Quietly by yourselves*

## Stop to think

What jobs do you hate, really hate?
What jobs do you like?

*When each child has had time to think*

## Share with one another

Why do you hate doing ..................... ?
Is it *when* you have to do it?
Is it *what* you have to do?
Is it *who* you have to do it for?
Who gets the good jobs?

*Welcome the Gospel. Sing Alleluia. (See page 106)*
*All stand (adapted from Mark 10:43-45)*

## Gospel

Jesus said,
"Anyone who follows me must do even horrible jobs for people if they want to be important."

This is the Gospel of the Lord.

**Praise be to you Lord Jesus Christ.**

*All sit*

## Let's chat  *(some suggestions)*

What jobs do you think James and John wanted?
Draw pictures of good jobs, not-so-bad jobs and horrible jobs.
Could you try a horrible job this week?

# Trust Jesus

## Welcome

## Let's sing and say (If celebrating the Introductory Rite 2, turn to page 105)

*Quietly by yourselves*

## Stop to think

Have you noticed that it gets dark earlier?
Do you like the dark?

*When each child has had time to think*

## Share with one another

What do you like/dislike about the dark?
What difference do the darker nights make?
Close your eyes, not too tight, so that you can keep them closed for a couple of minutes.
Promise?

## Light the Gospel candle

*Instead of a child a leader lights the candle.*
*Describe to the children what you are doing.*

Jesus his friends and a crowd of people were walking down the road when they heard someone shouting for help. It was a blind beggar called Bartimaeus. He kept shouting and some people told him to shut up.

*Welcome the Gospel. Sing Alleluia. (See page 106)*
*All stand (adapted from Mark 10:49-52)*

## Gospel

Jesus said,
   "Tell him to come here."
He jumped up, threw off his coat
and ran to Jesus.
Jesus said,
   "What can I do to help you?"
Bartimaeus said, "Let me see."
Jesus said,
   "You have trusted me, now you can see."
Bartimaeus could see
and he followed Jesus.

This is the Gospel of the Lord.
**Praise be to you Lord Jesus Christ.**

*All sit*

## Let's chat *(some suggestions)*

Open your eyes.
Who kept their eyes closed all the time?
What was it like not being able to see?
What do you think Bartimaeus wanted to see, to look at again?
Bartimaeus put his trust in Jesus.
Can you see Jesus?
Can you put your trust in him?

# The most important rule

## Welcome

## Let's sing and say

*(If celebrating the Introductory Rite 2, turn to page 105)*

*Quietly by yourselves*
## Stop to think

Hallowe'en is a very old word. When it was first used it was known as Hallow's Eve. Hollows means saints, eve means the day before. Hallows' Eve is the day before the feast of All Saints. Don't forget to celebrate that day too.

Ducking for apples is a traditional Hollows' Eve game. What are the rules for it? Which are the most important?

*When each child has had time to think*
## Share with one another

*Share your answers.*
Who keeps them in your family? Who breaks them? Why?
Do you agree what the rules are?
Do people sometimes say, 'I forgot'?
Sometimes there are so many rules that we do forget, sometimes we just pretend to forget.

## Light the Gospel candle

In Jesus' time there were lots of rules, almost too many to remember.
People would sometimes disagree about which rules were the most important.
One day a clever man came to Jesus to ask him which was the most important.

*Welcome the Gospel. Sing Alleluia. (See page 106)*
*All stand* *(adapted from Mark 12:29-31)*

### Gospel

This is what Jesus said,
"First, love God,
Second, love everyone else as much as you love yourself.
These are the most important rules."

This is the Gospel of the Lord.
**Praise be to you Lord Jesus Christ.**

*All sit*

## Let's chat  *(some suggestions)*

Explain the Gospel to the children.
Do you think it is right to love everyone?

# Be generous

## Welcome

## Let's sing and say   (If celebrating the Introductory Rite 2, turn to page 105)

*Quietly by yourselves*

## Stop to think

Do you share things at your parties? What?
Who shares with you? What?

*When each child has had time to think*

## Share with one another

*Share experiences and ask the children –*

What do you hate sharing with others? Why?
Is it easy to give away one sweet when you have ten or is it easier to give away your last sweet?

## Light the Gospel candle

Today we have a story about a woman who was brilliant at sharing.

*Welcome the Gospel. Sing Alleluia. (See page 106)*
*All stand*          *(adapted from Mark 12:38-44)*

### Gospel

 One day Jesus went into the temple and while he was there,
he saw all the people putting their money into the offerings box.

Some of the rich people put in a lot of money but then a poor old woman came along
and put in two little coins worth a penny.

Jesus saw this happen
and he said to his friends,
"That woman has put in more money than all the rest,
for they put in the money they had to spare,
but she has just put in everything she has."

*All sit*

### Let's chat   (some suggestions)

What do you think about that?
What would you say if you were there?
Where is your offerings box in Church?
Would you like to put something in next week?
Sometimes we are ashamed if we only have a little bit to give. We shouldn't be, every bit helps (remember the boy with the packed lunch?).

This is the Gospel of the Lord.

**Praise be to you Lord Jesus Christ.**

# Don't be afraid, I will come back again

## Welcome

## Let's sing and say
*(If celebrating the Introductory Rite 2, turn to page 105)*

*Quietly by yourselves*
## Stop to think
Who haven't you seen in a long time?
Why haven't you seen them?
Do you know when you will see them again?

*When each child has had time to think*
## Share with one another
Do you miss the people you haven't seen for a long time or do you forget them?
What did you do together?
Who surprises you with their visits? Do you like surprise visits?

*Welcome the Gospel. Sing Alleluia. (See page 106)*

*All stand (adapted from Mark 13:24-27, 32)*

---

### Gospel

One day Jesus told his friends,

"A time will come
when I will return and gather all my friends.
I will have great power
and we will all be together.
Nobody knows when this will happen,
only God our Father"

---

This is the Gospel of the Lord.
**Praise be to you Lord Jesus Christ.**

*All sit*
## Let's chat *(some suggestions)*
When would you like Jesus to come again? Why?
Perhaps you could draw a picture of – how you think Jesus will arrive;
what you think he will look like; what you will do; the people you think will be there.

# Christ the King

## Welcome

## Let's sing and say
*(If celebrating the Introductory Rite 2, turn to page 105)*

*Quietly by yourselves*

## Stop to think

Have you ever played 'Follow my leader'?
How do you play it?

*When each child has had time to think*

## Share with one another

*Play one quick game.*
*Ask a child to mime something Jesus did when he was here on earth.*
*Invite the others who wish to join in 'following the leader'.*

*When they're quiet:*

## Light the Gospel candle

Pilate was a Roman Leader. He was put in charge of lots of people.
He had to rule them like a King. He and the other Romans were bossy even though now and again they were helpful.

*Welcome the Gospel. Sing Alleluia. (See page 106)*
*All stand* *(adapted from John 18:33-37)*

### Gospel

Pilate said to Jesus,
"Are you a King?"
Jesus said, "Yes, but I am not a King like other Kings who rule people.
I am a King who is a leader,
and people choose to follow me."

This is the Gospel of the Lord.

**Praise be to you Lord Jesus Christ.**

*All sit*

## Let's chat *(some suggestions)*

Do you try to follow Jesus?
Would you like to make him your King?

# Let his glory be seen

## Welcome

## Let's sing and say *(If celebrating the Introductory Rite 1, turn to page 102)*

*Quietly by yourselves*

## Stop to think

This can be a boring time of year. What makes it boring?
What makes you bored, miserable, fed up, unhappy?
Do you know anyone who cheers you up?

*When each child has had time to think*

## Share with one another

*Share stories.*

We all feel bored and miserable at times. Probably because we spend too much time thinking about ourselves. If we did something for others we would soon cheer up and cheer others up too.

## Light the Gospel candle

We hear today how Jesus brings happiness to others at a wedding and for the first time showed a sign of the great things he could do for us.

*Welcome the Gospel. Sing Alleluia. (See page 104)*

*All stand* *(adapted from John 2:1-12)*

### Gospel

 Jesus, his mother and their friends were at a wedding when they ran out of wine.
Mary knew the bride and bridegroom would be disappointed.
She told Jesus what had happened.
She trusted him to do whatever was needed.
Later on Jesus told the waiter to fill the great jugs with water.
They did so but when they poured them out, they poured out wine not water.
He let his glory be seen and his friends began to believe.

This is the Gospel of the Lord.
**Praise be to you Lord Jesus Christ.**

*All sit*

### Let's chat *(some suggestions)*

Jesus wasn't just trying to do a clever trick.
He was showing us that he can change miserable times into happy times.
He can bring happiness.
If we put our trust in him like Mary and the waiter, if we do as he says, then we can find happiness.

Let's draw a jug. Fill your jugs with things that will bring happiness.

# Jesus shows us the way

## Welcome

## Let's sing and say (If celebrating the Introductory Rite 1, turn to page 102)

*Quietly by yourselves*

## Stop to think

What brings happiness? Think back to Christmas.
Yes, your presents brought you happiness but didn't you love everyone being in a good mood even more than your presents?

*When each child has had time to think*

## Share with one another

Has anyone ever said to you 'well done'? How does that make you feel?
Has anyone ever said to you 'thank you' or 'I'm glad you're my friend' or 'I love you'? How does that make you feel?

It's being put down, laughed at, bullied that makes us unhappy.

## Light the Gospel candle

Jesus went into the synagogue (church) to preach in his home town of Nazareth.

*Welcome the Gospel. Sing Alleluia. (See page 104)*
*All stand (adapted from Luke 1:4-21)*

## Gospel

Jesus said,

"I have come to give good news to the poor.
I have come to set free people who are being bullied.
I have come to help people who have been put down.
I have come to show a new way, to give new sight to the blind."

This is the Gospel of the Lord.
**Praise be to you Lord Jesus Christ.**

*All sit*

## Let's chat *(some suggestions)*

What would be good news to the poor?
How can we help Jesus in his work?
Remember we said we would help at our baptism.
Any ideas?

# Pointing out what's right

*Welcome*

*Let's sing and say* *(If celebrating the Introductory Rite 1, turn to page 102)*

*Quietly by yourselves*
## Stop to think
Have you ever stuck up for someone and then been laughed at for doing so?
Have you ever tried stopping someone from doing wrong and they have turned and called you names?
What sort of names do they call you?

*When each child has had time to think*
## Share with one another
*Share stories.*
Do others say 'who do you think you are?'
Do you find that you sometimes end up in trouble too?
Who are the children who usually get picked on, teased, laughed at?
What names are they called?

## Light the Gospel candle
Can you remember last week's Gospel?
(Read last week's Gospel again.)

*Welcome the Gospel. Sing Alleluia. (See page 104)*
*All stand* *(adapted from Luke 4:21-30)*

## Gospel

When Jesus finished reading out the important words everyone looked at him wondering what he was going to say next.

Jesus said, "I am going to do these things." The people got angry, "Who does he think he is?" they said.

Jesus told them to listen. But they wouldn't change their attitudes and they threw him out.

This is the Gospel of the Lord.

**Praise be to you Lord Jesus Christ.**

*All sit*
## Let's chat *(some suggestions)*
Was it easy for Jesus to stand up for what is right?
Do you think he got frightened?
What would you have done if you had been Jesus? Is it what Jesus did?
It's really hard to follow Jesus!
Jesus was actually in a lot of danger after they threw him out but he managed to escape. How do you think he escaped?

## Let's pray
Jesus please make us brave,
help us to do what's right.
In your loving way
hear our prayer.

# Don't be afraid, trust me

## Welcome

## Let's sing and say  *(If celebrating the Introductory Rite 1, turn to page 102)*

*Quietly by yourselves*

## Stop to think

Has anyone ever asked you to do something and you thought,
'that's stupid, that won't work.'
Has anyone ever said to you, 'this will do you good' and you think it won't?
Perhaps you had to take medicine or eat cabbage.
Has it ever happened to you?

*When each child has had time to think*

## Share with one another

*Share stories.*
Were you surprised when they turned out to be right?
How did you feel?
Are you still waiting to see if they are right?
Do you think they are?

## Light the Gospel candle

This week Jesus gives Peter a fishing hint. Peter has been a fisherman all his life and knows a lot about fishing but he still does as Jesus suggests.

*Welcome the Gospel. Sing Alleluia. (See page 104)*
*All stand*  *(adapted from Luke 5:1-11)*

### Gospel

 Jesus was talking to a crowd on the shore but there were so many people that they began to get in Jesus' way. He asked Peter if he could sit in his boat and talk to people from the lake. When Jesus had finished he said to Peter. "Try fishing over there." Peter told Jesus that he had been fishing all night and had caught nothing but he would try again.
This time Peter caught so many fish his nets almost broke.
Peter and his friends were amazed and they began to believe in Jesus.
They stared at him and Peter fell on his knees.
Jesus said, "Do not be afraid."
From then on they followed him.

This is the Gospel of the Lord. **Praise be to you Lord Jesus Christ.**

*All sit*

## Let's chat  *(some suggestions)*

What do you think about that?
It isn't easy to follow Jesus, to do as he says, remember last week's message.
It's hard to put your trust in people.
If we put our trust in Jesus we've nothing to be afraid of, 'something will turn up.'

# Trust in Jesus

## Welcome

## Let's sing and say  *(If celebrating the Introductory Rite 1, turn to page 102)*

*Quietly by yourselves*

## Stop to think

Has all the excitement of all the Christmas toys gone now?
What new toys would you like now?
Does your mum complain, 'want, want, want'?
Would you rather have a new toy or a good friend to play with,
a friend who would never boss you or run off to play with others?

*When each child has had time to think*

## Share with one another

What's your answer?
We all love having lots of new things but we know that after a while we get bored with them and that we want something else. We are never satisfied.
At the 'end of the day' we know that it's good company, friends and family that really pleases us or satisfies us. We are never bored or miserable when we have a friend.

## Light the Gospel candle

Jesus knows that we always want, want, want.
He also knows what will make us really happy.

*Welcome the Gospel. Sing Alleluia. (See page 104)*

*All stand*          *(adapted from Luke 6:20-23)*

## Gospel

 Jesus with Peter and the other men who had joined him sat down on the ground.
A large crowd joined them.
Jesus said,
 "Don't worry if you have very little, because one day you will have all that you need and more.
 But you, who have everything your things won't last for ever."

This is the Gospel of the Lord.

**Praise be to you Lord Jesus Christ.**

*All sit*

## Let's chat  *(some suggestions)*

What do you think that Jesus is telling us?
Do you think he's right?
The people had found a good friend in Jesus. He will always stick up for them.
We have found him too.

Let's put our trust in what he is saying about the way to real happiness.

# Love your enemies

## Welcome

## Let's sing and say (If celebrating the Introductory Rite 1, turn to page 102)

*Quietly by yourselves*

## Stop to think

Who do you love the most? Who do you love next to most?
Who else do you love? Who do you love not very much? Why?

*When each child has had time to think*

## Share with one another

It's hard to love people who hurt us or annoy us.
Everyone finds this very hard.
Do people love you? Do people love you all the time even when you're bad?

## Light the Gospel candle

The best news that Jesus ever told us was that *he loves us and God our Father loves us even when we are bad.*
That's great news.

*Welcome the Gospel. Sing Alleluia. (See page 104)*

*All stand* *(adapted from Luke 6:27-38)*

### Gospel

Jesus spoke to his friends,
"Listen.
Love your enemies.
Don't fight back.
Always be kind and loving
even to people who aren't kind to you.
Be just like God Our Father,
he is always kind to you,
and you will be happy."

This is the Gospel of the Lord.

**Praise be to you Lord Jesus Christ.**

*All sit*

### Let's chat *(some suggestions)*

This must be the hardest thing Jesus has asked us to do. He is really asking us to copy him.
He never stops loving us even when we do wicked things.
If we want to follow Jesus we must try to copy him and not stop loving people who upset us and make us angry.
It's difficult and Jesus understands and he won't stop loving us if we fail.
Are you going to give it a go this week?

Let's start by making friends with each other and offering each other the sign of peace.
*(For children it may be much more appropriate to link little fingers than shake hands. It's a sign often used by children when making friends after an argument.)*

# Take a look at yourself

## Welcome

### Let's sing and say    *(If celebrating the Introductory Rite 1, turn to page 102)*
*(or Introductory Rite 2, page 105)*

*Quietly by yourselves*

### Stop to think

Do you like people saying nice things about you?
How does it make you feel?
Do you like people moaning about you? How does it make you feel?

*When each child has had time to think*

### Share with one another

Do you know what the saying 'pot calling the kettle black' means?
Have you ever heard it said?
Explain the saying to the children.
We are all like this we often moan about others and forget that we are just as bad ourselves.

### Light the Gospel candle

Jesus noticed how often we were ready to be the pot calling the kettle black so he gave us another saying to remember.

*Welcome the Gospel. Sing Alleluia. (See page 104 and 106)*
*All stand (adapted from Luke 6:43-45)*

### Gospel

A good person sees what is good in others.

A bad person sees what is bad in others.

This is the Gospel of the Lord.

**Praise be to you Lord Jesus Christ.**

*All sit*

### Let's chat *(some suggestions)*

We are all good and bad. Sometimes we are one more than the other; we can choose. When we notice the good in others we bring out the goodness in ourselves.

# God helps everyone

## Welcome

## Let's sing and say *(If celebrating the Introductory Rite 2, turn to page 105)*

*Quietly by yourselves*

## Stop to think

When you are worried about someone or something who do you run to for help?
Who does your mum turn to? Who do the other members of your family turn to?
What about your friends?

*When each child has had time to think*

## Share with one another

Why do you turn to... ?
Why do you think your family and friends turn to... ?

## Light the Gospel candle

This week we hear about the soldier who turned to Jesus for help.

*Welcome the Gospel. Sing Alleluia. (See page 106)*
*All stand (adapted from Luke 7:1-10)*

### Gospel

There was once a Roman Soldier and he had a servant who was ill and dying. Now this servant was a very good servant so the Soldier sent some of his friends to ask Jesus if he would come and help him.

When these friends came to Jesus, they said, "This man has been very good to us. He has even built our meeting house for us."

So Jesus went along to the soldier's house and when he was nearly there, the soldier sent him another message, saying, "Please don't let me trouble you. I'm not good enough for you to come to me. But if you just tell my servant to be better then I'm sure he will be all right again.

You see I know you can do this because I am a soldier and I always do as I'm told. I also expect everyone else to do the same. If I say 'Go'.
Then people go where I tell them.
If I say 'Come here'.
Then they come to me.
If I say 'Do that'.
Then they get on with it at once.'

When Jesus heard this, he was surprised and very pleased.
"I haven't seen many people trust me like this," he said.
So he sent the messenger back to the soldier and when they got back they found the servant was already better.

A. J. McCallen

This is the Gospel of the Lord. **Praise be to you Lord Jesus Christ.**

*All sit*

## Let's chat *(some suggestions)*

What sort of person was the soldier? Do you know anyone like that?
What did Jesus think of him? Why do you think the soldier went to Jesus for help?
Why didn't he ask someone else?

# Jesus turns sadness into happiness

## Welcome

## Let's sing and say   *(If celebrating the Introductory Rite 2, turn to page 105)*

*Quietly by yourselves*

## Stop to think

Have you ever seen sad times turn into happy times?
Have you ever broken something and seen it repaired?
Have you ever lost anything and found it again?
Have you ever been sick and got better?
Has anyone ever left home and then come back again?
Has a friend ever left you and then come back?

*When each child has had time to think*

## Share with one another

Recall questions and share stories. If possible help the children to see that even in sad times people can laugh when they find something to hope for.

## Light the Gospel candle

This week we hear of someone's great sadness turning to joy.

*Welcome the Gospel. Sing Alleluia. (See page 106)*

*All stand (adapted from Luke 7:11-17)*

### Gospel

One day Jesus went to a place called Nain.
When he arrived he met a woman who was crying because her only son had died.
(Her husband was dead too and now she was all alone.)
She had just begun the funeral.
Jesus felt sorry for her,
he said, "Don't cry,"
and he stopped the funeral procession.
He went over to the boy and said,
"Young man I tell you get up,"
and the boy did.
His mother was so pleased and everyone praised Jesus.

*All sit*

### Let's chat   *(some suggestions)*

Have you any sadness that needs turning into happiness?
Give the children time to think of a prayer intention.
Let as many as possible say their intention out loud, after each intention say,

**Jesus turn our sadness into joy.**

*(Give the children a chance to make a private intention.)*

This is the Gospel of the Lord.
**Praise be to you Lord Jesus Christ.**

# Saying sorry

## Welcome

## Let's sing and say

(If celebrating the Introductory Rite 2, turn to page 105)

*Quietly by yourselves*

## Stop to think

Have you ever been forgiven for doing something that was wrong?
Have you ever said sorry?
Have you ever been forgiven without saying sorry?

*When each child has had time to think*

## Share with one another

Share stories.
Lots of things go wrong, by accident or on purpose.
We are often forgiven even if we don't say sorry.
When we really love the person, we want to say sorry.
The more we love them, the sooner we want to say sorry.

## Light the Gospel candle

Today we hear about a lady who couldn't wait to say sorry and a man who couldn't be bothered.

*Welcome the Gospel. Sing Alleluia. (See page 106)*

*All stand*          *(adapted from Luke 7:36-8)*

## Gospel

Jesus was invited to tea at Simon's house,
Simon was quite important and well to do.
While Jesus was eating his tea a woman came in and
went straight over to Jesus.
She couldn't wait to say sorry.

She knelt down in front of Jesus and cried.
She cried so much that her tears washed Jesus' feet.
She dried his feet with her hair and then rubbed perfume on them.

Jesus was very pleased with her
but Simon wasn't.
The woman had a bad name and
Simon didn't want her in his house or near Jesus.

Jesus saw that Simon wasn't pleased.
He said to Simon
'When I came to your house tonight you didn't make me welcome,
but this woman has, she is glad to see me.
She loves me.'

Then Jesus said to the woman
'Your sins are forgiven'.

This is the Gospel of the Lord.

**Praise be to you Lord Jesus Christ.**

*All sit*

## Let's chat  *(some suggestions)*

Simon didn't say sorry, the woman did. How did she say sorry?
Jesus didn't leave because Simon hadn't made him welcome or said sorry. He stayed and ate with Simon.
Do you think he was pleased to see the woman? How pleased?
Do you think they enjoyed each other's company?
Does Simon seem to enjoy Jesus' company?

Jesus loves Simon, Jesus loves the woman.
The woman left the house much happier than Simon.
Is it easy to say sorry?
Love means saying sorry.

*(N.B. Leaders, saying sorry is not a condition
of God's forgiveness,
God's forgiveness is always there.
It is a condition of our accepting his forgiveness).*

# Who am I?

*Welcome*

*Let's sing and say* *(If celebrating the Introductory Rite 2, turn to page 105)*

*Quietly by yourselves*

## Stop to think

Ask the children if they have read the story, "Ted and the Telephone"? It's a story about a boy who only half listens. He takes a message on the phone from his dad. Dad wants mum to meet him at the bank in Church Street. Ted tells mum that dad wants to meet her at the Church in Bank Street.

People are always telling us that we don't listen properly and they're right.
We too know that people don't listen to us. Have you ever tried explaining something to someone and they just don't understand:

- a birthday to an auntie or uncle?
- some new fashionable clothes, the sort that you like?
- a message from school about something you need?
- a message from home to school?
- something that's worrying you (it's often hard to find the words)?
- something that you desperately want to do?

*When each child has had time to think*

## Share with one another

How does it make you feel when you are not being understood?
How do you feel when people muddle you up with your brother, sister or cousin?

## Light the Gospel candle

This week we hear Jesus asking his friends a question. He's wondering if they have understood him. Only Peter seems to have the whole picture.

*Welcome the Gospel. Sing Alleluia. (See page 106)*

*All stand* *(adapted from Luke 9:18-24.)*

> ### Gospel
>
> Jesus said to his friends,
> "Who do the crowds say-that I am?"
> His friends answered,
> "Some say John the Baptist (Jesus' cousin),
> others say Elijah (a great teacher and wise man)."
> Jesus turned to his friends and said,
> "Who do you say I am?"
> Peter answered, "You are God's Son."

This is the Gospel of the Lord. **Praise be to you Lord Jesus Christ.**

*All sit*

## Let's chat *(some suggestions)*

Jesus there are lots of things we don't understand. We get things muddled, but we do love you. Please help us to understand.
*(Give the children time, or quiet private prayer about their own muddles.)*

# Put God's work first

## Welcome

## Let's sing and say  (If celebrating the Introductory Rite 2, turn to page 105)

*Quietly by yourselves*

## Stop to think

Do you like being interrupted

- called in early from play
- asked to go on a message
- told to do a job
- told to look after your brother/sister?

Mum and dad hate being interrupted too.
When you ask if you can go out to play or go to... (wherever); does your mum say 'when you have finished your tea' or 'after you have finished your homework'?
If you moan she may say 'first things first'. What does she mean?

*When each child has had time to think*

## Share with one another

*Share stories.*
What does 'First things first' mean? What is really first? What should be?

## Light the Gospel candle

This week Jesus is telling us to put his work first.

*Welcome the Gospel. Sing Alleluia. (See page 106)*

*All stand (adapted from Luke 9:57-62)*

### Gospel

 Jesus was walking along the road when a man came up to him and said
"I will follow you wherever you go."

Jesus met some others and invited them to follow him,
but they said,
"Later when I have taken care of things at home,
there's one or two things I need to do."

Jesus said "You must put God's work first."

*All sit*

### Let's chat *(some suggestions)*

What do you think they had to do at home?
Can you put God's work first at home?
How can you put God's work first?
Perhaps we can listen to the interruptions?

This is the Gospel of the Lord.
**Praise be to you Lord Jesus Christ.**

# Peace to this house

## Welcome

## Let's sing and say *(If celebrating the Introductory Rite 2, turn to page 105)*

*Quietly by yourselves*

## Stop to think

Do you like going on jobs?
What kind of jobs?
Do you like to have a friend or partner with you? Why?

*When each child has had time to think*

## Share with one another

Why do you like to take a friend with you?
What kind of things do you need to take with you when you go on a job?

## Light the Gospel candle

This week we learn that Jesus sent seventy two friends on a job. They went in twos. (How many pairs does that make?) Find a partner, stand in twos to hear the Gospel.

*Welcome the Gospel. Sing Alleluia. (See page 106)*
*All stand    (adapted from Luke 10:1-12, 17-20)*

---

### Gospel

 Jesus picked seventy two friends and put them in pairs.
He sent them on a message and told them they didn't need to take things with them.
They were to visit as many people as they could.
When the people invited them in they were to say,
"Peace be to this house."

*(Stop the reading ask the children to offer each other a sign of peace. When they have settled tell them to sit and continue the gospel).*

Jesus said
"You are to stay wherever you are made welcome,
eat whatever you are given and help make the sick better.
If people don't make you welcome, don't stay."

When the seventy two came back they were full of stories
about the wonderful time they had had.

Jesus told them even better news he said,
"I'm glad that you are happy,
but be happier still
because your names are written in heaven."

---

This is the Gospel of the Lord. **Praise be to you Lord Jesus Christ.**

*All sit*

## Let's chat *(some suggestions)*

What would be the good times that the seventy two had to talk about? Do you think they were happier with Jesus' news?

How would you feel going on such a message? Your names are written in heaven (baptism). When you go back to Church (in twos) remember to give as many people as you can the sign of peace.

# The unexpected helper

## Welcome

## Let's sing and say  *(If celebrating the Introductory Rite 2, turn to page 105)*

*Quietly by yourselves*
## Stop to think

Who is always picked for jobs? Why? Are you often picked for jobs? Why?
What kind of jobs are you given? Which ones do you like?

*When each child has had time to think*
## Share with one another

*Share experiences.*
Do you ever look out for jobs, or do jobs without being asked?

## Light the Gospel candle

This week Jesus tells us a story. Three people get a chance to do a job.
Everyone expects the first two will do it but they don't. It's the third person who nobody
expects to help who does the job perfectly.

*Welcome the Gospel. Sing Alleluia. (See page 106)*
*Suitable for mime (adapted from Luke 10:29-37)*

## Gospel

 One day, Jesus told this story:
There was once a man who was going from Jerusalem to Jericho and he was attacked by bandits.

They tore off his clothes and beat him up, leaving him half dead on the road.

A few minutes later, a priest went down the same road but he didn't stop to help the poor man he went straight past on the other side of the road.

Then a teacher came along as well but he hurried past in the same way.

Then a stranger came.
He felt sorry for the poor man so he went across to him.
He bandaged up his wounds, then he put him over his horse and took him to a hotel and looked after him all night.

Next morning he had to go away again so he left enough money for the man to stay a bit longer in the hotel, and he promised to come back later and pay the bill.
Then Jesus said,
"That's what I call a real friend."

A. J. McCallen

This is the Gospel of the Lord.
**Praise be to you Lord Jesus Christ.**

*All sit*

## Let's chat  *(some suggestions)*

Could you be an unexpected helper this week?
Try to do a job that you have not done before.

# The important things

## Welcome

## Let's sing and say *(If celebrating the Introductory Rite 2, turn to page 105)*

*Quietly by yourselves*

## Stop to think

Do you manage to be an unexpected helper? Do you sometimes moan when it's your turn to do a job, saying 'it's not my turn' or 'our hasn't done any jobs'?
Do your sisters and brothers moan about you?

*When each child has had time to think*

## Share with one another

*Share experiences.*

Do you run to your mum and say, 'make her/him help me'?
Sometimes we moan because they have a job we want. We say, 'it's not fair.
I haven't had a turn'. We all moan and spend too much time watching what each other does. A great many arguments are started this way.

## Light the Gospel candle

This week Jesus shows us what's really important.

*Welcome the Gospel. Sing Alleluia. (See page 106)*

*All stand        (adapted from Luke 10:38-42)*

### Gospel

Jesus went to a village to visit some friends Martha and Mary. Martha invited him in and began to get food ready for Jesus whilst Mary sat and listened to Jesus.

Martha soon began to moan and said to Jesus, "Tell Mary to help me."
Jesus said "Martha don't make such a fuss about things that don't matter. It's the love that we show each other that matters and that's the job that Mary is doing."

This is the Gospel of the Lord. **Praise be to you Lord Jesus Christ.**

*All sit*

## Let's chat *(some suggestions)*

Do you think Jesus was fair?
Martha was showing love by getting the food ready.
Mary was showing love by listening to Jesus.
Martha spoilt it by moaning. She made too much fuss.

*(Leaders: Jesus always goes beyond fairness or justice. He calls us to greater love which is mercy).*

We all spend our day fussing about too many things.
Let's try and find time to be still and pray to Jesus.
What's the best time of day for you to pray?

# Teach us to pray

## Welcome

### Let's sing and say  (If celebrating the Introductory Rite 2, turn to page 105)

*Quietly by yourselves*

### Stop to think

When you are stuck who do you turn to for help?
When you are stuck with sums?
When you are stuck with learning to swim or to ride a bike?
When you are stuck, not knowing what kind of birthday present to buy?

*When each child has had time to think*

### Share with one another

*Share experiences.*
When we are stuck we usually turn to whoever we are sure will have the answer and who we know will help us.

### Light the Gospel candle

Jesus' friends were stuck. They wanted to be better at praying.

*Welcome the Gospel. Sing Alleluia. (See page 106)*
*All stand (adapted from Luke 11:1-14)*

---

### Gospel

One day Jesus was saying his prayers
and when he had finished one of his friends said, "Teach us to pray."
So Jesus told them to say this prayer.

"Father,
we want everyone to praise you,
and we want your kingdom to grow
better and better
until it is perfect.
Give us enough food each day
forgive us when we go wrong,
just as we forgive others
when they do wrong to us,
and help us when we are put to the test."

A. J. McCallen

This is the Gospel of the Lord.
**Praise be to you Lord Jesus Christ.**

*All sit*

### Let's chat  (some suggestions)

What do you think about that prayer?
Do you like it?
Which is your favourite part?
Shall we learn it?

# The greedy man

*Welcome*

*Let's sing and say* (If celebrating the Introductory Rite 2, turn to page 105)

*Quietly by yourselves*

## Stop to think

Have you a collection of any kind or do you think collecting things is a waste of time?
What other things do you think are a waste of time?

*When each child has had time to think*

## Share with one another

Share ideas about what you think is a waste of time. It can be good fun collecting things
but the fun can go if we are fussy about who looks at or touches our things.
We might keep our things that way, but we won't keep our friends.
What would you rather have things or friends? What is a good use of time?

## Light the Gospel candle

Today we hear a story about a busy man.
Do you think he uses his time wisely?

*Welcome the Gospel. Sing Alleluia. (See page 106)*

*All stand (adapted from Luke 12:16-21)*

### Gospel

 Jesus said,
"There once was a rich man
who had so many things
that he couldn't fit them all in his house.

The man decided to build a bigger house.
When he had built his house he was
pleased with himself.
He thought now I will take it easy.

God said, 'Fool! What happens if you die
tonight? What good will all this be to you?' "

This is the Gospel of the Lord.

**Praise be to you Lord Jesus Christ.**

*All sit*

### Let's chat  (some suggestions)

What use would the man's things be to
him if he died?
Did the man use his time wisely?
What was he worrying about?
What kind of man was he?
What things do we really need to keep
us alive?

# Be ready

## Welcome

## Let's sing and say *(If celebrating the Introductory Rite 2, turn to page 105)*

*Quietly by yourselves*

## Stop to think

Are you ever late? Who in your family is always the last one to be ready?
Have you ever missed a bus, a train, or the start of something because you weren't ready on time?

*When each child has had time to think*

## Share with one another

We are often late because we don't notice time slipping by.
This week we hear that we are chosen. God has something special for us.
He wants us to have the kingdom.
Are you ready for it? We don't have to move to live in the kingdom. To have the kingdom we just have to change our ways to God's ways. Then we will have made God our King.
We will have his kingdom. It will take a long time. *(This may be a difficult idea for the children to grasp. Only attempt to explain if you think they are able to understand).*

## Light the Gospel candle

*Welcome the Gospel. Sing Alleluia. (See page 106)*

*All stand     (adapted from Luke 12:32-34, 40)*

### Gospel

 Jesus said to his friends,
"There is no need to be afraid little flock.
God is pleased with you
and he wants you to have the kingdom."
Give things away and spend your time being good
because this will last for ever.
People can steal your things
but they can't steal your goodness.
Always be busy at this job
and watch out for me.
I will come back so be ready."

This is the Gospel of the Lord.

**Praise be to you Lord Jesus Christ.**

*All sit*

### Let's chat  *(some suggestions)*

We will have the kingdom when we have happiness. We are all happy when we are good to each other.
We will enjoy the kingdom, no greedy people, no fighting, no calling names, no tormenting, no shouting.
Don't let time slip by.
Don't be late and miss your chances.
Get busy now.

Let's start by making friends (children's sign of peace).
When we go back to church we will make friends with everyone.
Keep busy spreading happiness all day and what a happy day you'll have.

# Ups and downs

## Welcome

## Let's sing and say (If celebrating the Introductory Rite 2, turn to page 105)

*Quietly by yourselves*

## Stop to think

What's been the best part of the holidays?
What's been the worst part of the holidays?

*When each child has had time to think*

## Share with one another

*Share experiences.*

Life is full of 'ups and downs'. What are the ups? What are the downs?
Explain to the children the saying 'take the rough with the smooth'.

## Light the Gospel candle

Welcome the Gospel. Sing Alleluia. (See page 106)

*All stand* (adapted from Luke 12:51-53)

> **Gospel**
>
> Jesus is telling us
> that we have to take the rough with the smooth.
> Jesus said,
> "It won't be easy following me,
> not everyone will agree with you."

This is the Gospel of the Lord.
**Praise be to you Lord Jesus Christ.**

*All sit*

## Let's chat (some suggestions)

Has anyone ever laughed at you, called you names because you have done what you know is right?
Do people sometimes think you are daft because you give things away?
Do people think you are a coward because you walk away from a fight?
Do people think that you have 'gone soft' because you won't join in name calling?

# The last will be first and the first will be last

## Welcome

## Let's sing and say *(If celebrating the Introductory Rite 2, turn to page 105)*

*Quietly by yourselves*

## Stop to think

Have you ever been 'beaten to it' because you have been too slow or too dozy to take your chance

- missed a bargain?
- missed a part in a school play or assembly?
- missed a good trip out with your mum because you couldn't be bothered to leave the TV?

*When each child has had time to think*

## Share with one another

We all have lots of chances and we must be ready to take them. Explain the saying 'first come first served.'

## Light the Gospel candle

Jesus is telling us to take care and not to miss our chance.

*Welcome the Gospel. Sing Alleluia. (See page 106)*

*All stand*      *(adapted from Luke 13:22-30)*

### Gospel

Jesus was on his way to Jerusalem when someone stopped him and asked, "How many people will belong in the Kingdom?" Jesus said,
 "Lots of people,
 people from all over the world,
 so don't leave it too late
 or they will all find happiness before you."

This is the Gospel of the Lord.
**Praise be to you Lord Jesus Christ.**

*All sit*

### Let's chat *(some suggestions)*

Does this mean we have to push our way to the front?
What does it mean?
Are you glad that everyone can belong to the kingdom?

Explain 'The last will be first and the first will be last'.

# Don't be so high and mighty

*Welcome*

*Let's sing and say* *(If celebrating the Introductory Rite 2, turn to page 105)*

*Quietly by yourselves*

**Stop to think**

Why do people think they are more important than others?
Is it because they are

- stronger,   • clever         • richer,
- funny,      • good looking?

What do you think makes someone important?

*When each child has had time to think*

**Share with one another**

*Share thoughts.*
Explain to the children the saying, 'There's always someone better than yourself'.

**Light the Gospel candle**

*Welcome the Gospel. Sing Alleluia. (See page 106)*
*All stand (adapted from Luke 14:1, 7-14)*

### Gospel

 Jesus had been invited to a meal at a very important man's house. He noticed how everyone rushed to have the best places.
He said, "When you are invited to a party, don't take the best place because someone much more important than you may have been invited.
When you have to change your place you will feel very embarrassed.
Always sit in the unimportant place then you might be asked to move to the important place."
Jesus hadn't finished. He had more to say.
"When you have a party don't just invite people who invite you back, invite those who can't invite you back."

This is the Gospel of the Lord.
**Praise be to you Lord Jesus Christ.**

*All sit*

**Let's chat** *(some suggestions)*

What is Jesus telling us today?
Is he just talking about parties?
What else is he talking about?

**Let's pray**

Jesus please help us
to always put others first.

Lord hear us, **Lord please hear us.**

# It isn't easy

## *Welcome*

## *Let's sing and say* *(If celebrating the Introductory Rite 2, turn to page 105)*

*Quietly by yourselves*

## Stop to think

Have you ever been determined to
• get something right,
• learn to ride a bike,
• learn to swim,
• learn a dance?

*When each child has had time to think*

## Share with one another

Did you manage it in the end? Was it really difficult?
When was it hardest? How long did it take you?

When we are determined to tackle something we keep working at it until we have it right.
It can take up a lot of our time, but if we are really determined we think about little else,
nothing else seems important.

## Light the Gospel candle

Jesus is telling us this week that following him isn't easy, but if we are really determined
nothing else seems to matter.

*Welcome the Gospel. Sing Alleluia. (See page 106)*

*All stand (adapted from Luke 14:25-33)*

| Gospel | there are plenty of hard times ahead. |
|---|---|
|  Crowds of people followed Jesus as he went from place to place. He said to them, "Following me isn't easy | If you're really determined then you will put everything else into second place. Think about this. Are you sure you want to try? If you do, you must put me first." |

This is the Gospel of the Lord. **Praise be to you Lord Jesus Christ.**

*All sit*

## Let's chat *(some suggestions)*

Jesus is not kidding is he?
It certainly is hard. Most of the time we can't do what he has asked of us.
What's the hardest to do?
Let's try one thing only this week. Let's really try to share.
It will be tough but as a song says, 'When the going gets tough, the tough get going'.

# God loves us even when we go wrong

## Welcome

## Let's sing and say

*(If celebrating the Introductory Rite 2, turn to page 105)*

*Quietly by yourselves*

## Stop to think

Have you ever lost anything that was really important to you?

*(Give the children plenty of time)*

*When each child has had time to think*

## Share with one another

Did you hunt and hunt and hunt until you found it?
Never giving up?
Were you upset to lose it?
Were you glad to find it? How did you feel?
Did anyone help you?

## Light the Gospel candle

This week Jesus tells us a story about a father who thought he had lost his son forever, but he came home.

*Welcome the Gospel. Sing Alleluia. (See page 106)*

*All stand. Perhaps this could be mimed (adapted from Luke 15:11-24)*

## Gospel

One day Jesus told his friends this story.

There was once a farmer who had two sons.
The younger son came to his father and said;
"Isn't it about time that you gave me my share of the farm?"
So the father gave him his share of the money.
A few days later, the boy packed his bags and left home.
He went a long way away and he had a good time,
but he wasted all his money until at last he didn't even have enough to buy something to eat.
So he had to get a job on a farm feeding the pigs, and he was so hungry, he would even have eaten the pig-swill if he could have got it.

Then he began to think "What a fool am I," he said to himself.
"Even the men who only work for my father have as much as they want to eat.
And here am I, starving to death.
I know I have hurt God and I've hurt my father but I'm going back home.
I'll tell my father I am sorry and I'll ask him to give me a job as a workman because I'm not good enough to be called his son anymore".

So he went home again and his father saw him coming.
He felt sorry for the boy and ran out to meet him and made him welcome.

The boy began to say, "I have done wrong..."
But his father didn't wait for him to finish.
He told his servant to get out some good clothes for the boy and get a meal ready.

"I thought I had lost my boy," he said.
"I thought he was dead.
But now he is alive again
and I have found him once more."

A. J. McCallen

This is the Gospel of the Lord.
**Praise be to you Lord Jesus Christ.**

*All sit*

## Let's chat *(some suggestions)*

The father in this story is just like God and the boy just like us.
We do wrong but just like the Father, God doesn't mind he just wants us back.
Why did the boy want to come back home? (Because he was hungry)
Do you think he was glad to be back?
How do you think the father felt?
Did the father even let the boy say what he had done wrong?

If there's time tell the rest of the story (the reaction of the older brother).
Point out that the Father seems to be having a bad time with both his sons but that he still has a party even though the situation isn't perfect.
God does not insist on perfection. He just wants us to be with him.

# Let nothing get in the way of loving God

## Welcome

### Let's sing and say  (If celebrating the Introductory Rite 2, turn to page 105)

*Quietly by yourselves*
### Stop to think

Can you do two things at once?

*When each child has had time to think*
### Share with one another

*(If they claim to be able to, let them show you. Ask the children to pat their head with one hand and rub their tummy with the other at the same time.)*

See it's very difficult. If you do one well, you make a mess of the other.
You have to choose which to do.

### Light the Gospel candle

Jesus this week is telling us that we really can't do two things at once properly.
We have to choose.

*Welcome the Gospel. Sing Alleluia. (See page 106)*
*All stand*          *(adapted from Luke 16:13)*

---

### Gospel

 No one can do two things well at the same time.
You will do well at one and make a mess of the other.

If you spend your life making money, thinking about money and loving money all the time you will forget God.

---

This is the Gospel of the Lord. **Praise be to you Lord Jesus Christ.**

*All sit*

### Let's chat *(some suggestions)*

If you spend all your time thinking about money what kind of person might you become?
Is that kind of person serving God?
Does God want us to do without money?
Of course not, we need it. He is trying to say to us that if we make it the first most important thing in our life soon we will forget him.
Would you like to put some money in the box in church?
Don't worry if you only have a penny to give, whoever gets it will be pleased.

# Remember the poor

*Welcome*

*Let's sing and say* (If celebrating the Introductory Rite 2, turn to page 105)

*Quietly by yourselves*

## Stop to think

When you see very hungry people (on TV) asking for help, how do you feel?
What would you like to do?

*When each child has had time to think*

## Share with one another

*(Give the children time to share their feelings. Share yours too.)*
As soon as we see them we want to send them money and so we should.
The trouble is that we may not have very much money to send because we may have spent it on things we don't need.
We buy clothes and throw them away before they are worn out. We buy toys and things that we hardly ever play with or use. We waste so much of our money.
We want the best of everything, but if we take the best of everything who gets the worst?

## Light the Gospel candle

Today Jesus gives us a story that really makes us think.

*Welcome the Gospel. Sing Alleluia. (See page 106)*
*All stand (adapted from Luke 16:19-31)*

## Gospel

Jesus told this story.
There was once a very rich man who had the best of everything.
Outside his house there was a very poor sick man called Lazarus who would have loved to have anything the man threw away.

Lazarus died and went to heaven where he was very happy.

The rich man died too and he could see Lazarus was happy.
He wasn't happy and he wanted Lazarus to cheer him up.

God said, "He cannot help you. You have had lots of happy times now it's Lazarus' turn."

The rich man wished he had helped Lazarus when he was alive but he was too late now that he was dead.

This is the Gospel of the Lord.
**Praise be to you Lord Jesus Christ.**

*All sit*

## Let's chat *(some suggestions)*

*(Try and help the children to see that it isn't just about giving money to the poor.*
*It's really about us changing our attitude to possessions)*

What can we do to help the poor?

Explain the saying, 'Don't put off until tomorrow what you can do today'.

What can we do today? (Be happy with everything we have).

Remember if we have the best of everything, many others have to take second best and a great many people are left with the worst.

# Have faith

## Welcome

## Let's sing and say  *(If celebrating the Introductory Rite 2, turn to page 105)*

*Quietly by yourselves*

## Stop to think

Have you ever watched Record Breakers on TV?
Have you ever heard of the Guinness Book of Records?
What is the most amazing thing you have ever seen or heard?

*When each child has had time to think*

## Share with one another

Share amazing facts. Are you extraordinary?
Look at each other, there are no two people exactly alike. You could travel the world and never find anyone exactly like you, even though there are millions and millions of people. There are also millions and millions of different kind of animals.
We hardly ever bump into each other because the world is so big. But if we think the world is big what about space? Who made all of this?

## Light the Gospel candle

Jesus is telling us this week that if we put our trust in him we can do extraordinary things.

*Welcome the Gospel. Sing Alleluia. (See page 106)*
*All stand*          *(adapted from Luke 17:5-10)*

### Gospel

 One day Jesus' friends said to him, "Increase our faith."

*(What do you think they meant?)*

Jesus said,
  "if your faith was a small as a speck
  you would be able to do amazing things."
He then said,
  "Don't just be happy to do ordinary things,
  do extraordinary things. Be extra good to
  people".

This is the Gospel of the Lord.
**Praise be to you Lord Jesus Christ.**

*All sit*

## Let's chat  *(some suggestions)*

What do you think Jesus' friends meant when they asked him to 'increase our faith.'?
What amazing things would you like to do?
What extraordinary good things would you like to do?
Would they be possible or impossible for you to do? Why?

## Let's pray

Jesus when we are frightened
when we have to face something difficult
when we just don't know what to do
help us to put our trust in you.

# Thanks be to God

## Welcome

## Let's sing and say
(If celebrating the Introductory Rite 2, turn to page 105)

*Quietly by yourselves*

## Stop to think

Have you ever been so sick that you
couldn't play with other children?
Did other children have to keep away in
case they caught your sickness?
Were you very lonely?
Did some people ever call you names
(spotty face)?

*When each child has had time to think*

## Share with one another

Share feelings of loneliness and rejection.
How long did it take for you to get better?
How did you feel when it was all over?

## Light the Gospel candle

This week we hear what happened when Jesus met ten sick people who thought that they
would never get better; until they met Jesus.

*Welcome the Gospel. Sing Alleluia. (See page 106)*

*All stand*      *(adapted from Luke 17:11-1 )*

*Gospel*     (perhaps this could be mimed)

One day Jesus went up to Jerusalem and
while he was on his way, he went into a
little town nearby.

Ten lepers came out to meet him there,
and they moved across to him, saying,
"Please help us, Jesus."

When he saw them, Jesus said,
  "Go and see the priest."
So they did, and as they were on their way,
they were healed.

*(What do you think would be the first thing they would do?*
*Many of the children will suggest seeing family and friends and will also forget to suggest*
*thanks. Don't point this out yet.)*

One of the ten came straight back to Jesus
and he praised God at the top of his voice,
throwing himself down in front of Jesus.
"Thank you, Jesus," he said, "Thank you very much."

Jesus then said,
  "Didn't all the others get better as well?
  Or have they just not bothered to come and say thank you?
  I wonder why you are the only one who came back.
  Stand up my friend", he said.
  "God loves you for what you have done."

A. J. McCallen

This is the Gospel of the Lord.

**Praise be to you Lord Jesus Christ.**

*All sit*

## Let's chat *(some suggestions)*

How glad do you think the lepers were to see Jesus?
What did they do that showed they believed that Jesus could make them well? Why do you
think only one came back to say thanks?
Jesus doesn't seem to be thanked too often. Do we forget to thank him?

Say thanks: Say some thank-you prayers to God.
For ................................. thank you.
Think of the people we take for granted.
Make a list of who you would like to thank today.

# Don't give up

## Welcome

## Let's sing and say *(If celebrating the Introductory Rite 2, turn to page 105)*

*Quietly by yourselves*
## Stop to think

When you play 'I spy' or some other such game are you the first to give up when you can't find the answer, or do you say you'll never give up?
Do you give up easily at everything, just sometimes or never?

*When each child has had time to think*
## Share with one another

Share experiences of giving up.
When you pray for something do you sometimes give up? Why?
Sometimes when we pray for something it's hard to understand why God doesn't give us what we want or need.

Have you ever seen a mum make a bottle for a baby? Sometimes when she makes it it's so hot that it would burn the baby so she cools it in a jug of water. The baby is very hungry and cries and screams for food.
She can see the bottle and thinks that mum is very unkind and even cruel not to give her what she wants and really needs.
Is mum cruel? When will mum feed the baby?
The baby doesn't understand, can't understand (she's too young) that the bottle is too hot.

We are like the baby when we pray. We often pray for good things that we need.
If God doesn't answer our prayer perhaps it's because the time is not right or it's really not for the best. We must put our trust in God even though like the baby we don't and can't understand.

## Light the Gospel candle

Jesus is telling us this week to never give up.

*Welcome the Gospel. Sing Alleluia. (See page 106)*

*All stand*        *(adapted from Luke 18:1-8)*

### Gospel

Jesus told this story.
There once was a judge. He wasn't a good judge. He was often unfair.
A woman came to see him to ask him to sort out her problem with her enemy.
The judge didn't bother.
The woman went the next day and asked again.
He still didn't do anything about her problem.
The woman kept asking, everyday.
In the end the judge said "This woman is a pest,
I'll never get any peace until I give her what she wants."

Then Jesus said,
   "If an unfair judge can give the woman what she wants
   just think what God would give you if you ask.
   Don't give up."

This is the Gospel of the Lord.

**Praise be to you Lord Jesus Christ.**

*All sit*

### Let's chat  *(some suggestions)*

What do you think about the woman?
Do you think she ever got tired and wanted to give up?
Is there anything you have given up on?
Perhaps you would like to try again.
Pray very quietly in your mind.
Ask God to help you not to give up.

# We are all sinners

*Welcome*

*Let's sing and say*   (If celebrating the Introductory Rite 2, turn to page 105)

*Quietly by yourselves*

### Stop to think

What does boasting mean? How do people behave when they are boasting?
What do you think is the opposite to boasting?
How do people behave when they are not boasting?

*When each child has had time to think*

### Share with one another

Share your answers. How do you feel about people who boast?
Are they always as good as they say?

### Light the Gospel candle

Jesus told a story about two men who went to the temple to stand and praise God.
Listen carefully. Be ready to decide.
Who do you think really praised God?

*Welcome the Gospel. Sing Alleluia. (See page 106)*
*All stand*          *(adapted from Luke 18:9-14)*

---

### Gospel

Jesus said,
"Two men went to church to pray.
One man was an important leader.
The other man collected money for the government
and he often cheated people asking for more money than he should.
When they arrived the important man stood up proudly and said,
"Thank you God that I am a good man and not like everyone else,
especially that man over there who cheats.
I do so many good things."

The man who collected money for the government was far away from the important man.
He was saying his prayers too but he hung his head in shame,
"God I'm sorry please forgive me," was his prayer.

*All sit*

### Let's chat   *(some suggestions)*

Who do you think pleased God?
We need to remember that we are all sinners and not be so quick to find fault in others.
It may be that you can do amazing things at your Halloween celebrations this week (or whenever) but why not stand back and let others show you just how clever they can be.

Remember to praise them and to thank everyone.
*(Recall the Gospel two weeks ago).*
In our excitement we may forget.

This is the Gospel of the Lord.
**Praise be to you Lord Jesus Christ.**

# Making a new start

## Welcome

## Let's sing and say (If celebrating the Introductory Rite 2, turn to page 105)

*Quietly by yourselves*

## Stop to think

Have you ever heard anyone say, 'I don't care'?
Sometimes they say it when they have done something wrong or when they have fallen out of friends with someone.
Sometimes they mean it, sometimes they don't.

*When each child has had time to think*

## Share with one another

Have you ever heard it said?
Do people sometimes change their minds?
Why do they change their minds and begin to care?

## Light the Gospel candle

This week we hear that Jesus met a man who cheated people and the man didn't seem to care. Listen to see if he changes his mind.

*Welcome the Gospel. Sing Alleluia. (See page 106)*

*All stand*        *(adapted from Luke 19:1-10)*

### Gospel

One day, Jesus went to Jericho. Now a man lived there called Zacchaeus and he was very rich, because he collected money for the Romans. This man was very keen to see what Jesus looked like, but he was only little, and he couldn't see anything with all the people there.

So he ran on in front, and climbed up a sycamore tree just to see Jesus when he went past.

But Jesus saw him up the tree and said, "Come down, I want to stay in your house today." So Zacchaeus climbed down as quickly as he could, and took him home.

Everyone else complained and said, "He's a bad man, Jesus shouldn't have gone there." But Zacchaeus said "Look Jesus, I'm going to give half of everything I've got to the poor. And if I've cheated anyone I'll give him back four times as much as I took."

A. J. McCallen

This is the Gospel of the Lord. **Praise be to you Lord Jesus Christ.**

*All sit*

## Let's chat (some suggestions)

Do you think Jesus should have gone to stay at Zacchaeus' house? Why?
In the beginning Zacchaeus doesn't seem to care that he has cheated people.

Does he care at the end of the story?
What changed his mind?
Perhaps you could draw Zacchaeus:
saying, 'I don't care' saying,
        'I do care'.

# All questions will be answered

## Welcome

At this time of year we remember people who have died.
Do you know anyone who has died? Let's pray for them.

## Prayer

God our Father
we pray for our family and friends who have died.
They are on their way to live with you now
and we know they will be very happy.
Help them on their journey.
Give them our love, we miss them
but we look forward to the day
when we shall be with them and you in heaven.
Amen.

## Let's sing and say (If celebrating the Introductory Rite 2, turn to page 105)

*Quietly by yourselves*

## Stop to think

Is there anything that you wonder about?
Anything at all?
Are there questions that you have never found an answer to?

*When each child has had time to think*

## Share with one another

Let the children ask their questions and don't attempt to answer them all.
Leave lots of unanswered questions and add a few of your own.

## Light the Gospel candle

*Welcome the Gospel. Sing Alleluia. (See page 106)*
*All stand*     (adapted from Luke 20:27-28)

### Gospel

Some people came to Jesus to ask lots of questions.
They wanted to know what happens when we die.
"Do we still have the same relations?"
Jesus said,
"When we get to heaven we will all be together and all our questions will be answered."

This is the Gospel of the Lord.
**Praise be to you Lord Jesus Christ.**

*All sit*

### Let's chat *(some suggestions)*

Let's say today's prayer again.

Perhaps you might draw Jesus with all your family and friends who have died.

# Things don't last forever

## Welcome

It's November and this is the time of year that we especially remember and pray for all those who have died. (see page 213)

## Let's sing and say (If celebrating the Introductory Rite 2, turn to page 105)

*Quietly by yourselves*

## Stop to think

What might only last a day?
What might only last a week?
What might only last a year?
What will last longer?
Will anything last forever?

*When each child has had time to think*

## Share with one another

Repeat the questions and see what answers the children come up with.
What sort of things would you like to be over quickly?
What sort of things would you like to last forever?
Everything seems to come to an end.

## Light the Gospel candle

*Welcome the Gospel. Sing Alleluia.* (See page 106)
*All stand*

### Gospel

 Jesus said,
"Look around you
all this will come to an end and be forgotten.
But you won't.
You and your goodness will be remembered
and you will live forever."

This is the Gospel of the Lord.
**Praise be to you Lord Jesus Christ.**

*All sit*

## Let's chat *(some suggestions)*

What would you like to be remembered for?

# Christic the King

*Christ the King*

## Welcome

Did you know that today is the last Sunday of the Church's year?
It is not the last Sunday of the year, there are about five more, but it is the last in the Church's year.

## Let's sing and say  *(If celebrating the Introductory Rite 2, turn to page 105)*

*Quietly by yourselves*

## Stop to think

What has happened to the hardest jobs that Jesus has given us this year?

- loving people who hate us?
- giving away money and other things?
- not always taking the best of everything?
- no boasting?
- saying sorry?
- helping others?

Can you think of any others?

*When each child has had time to think*

## Share with one another

Which do you think is the hardest?
*(Leaders say which you find the hardest.)*
Jesus always knew it would be hard. He found it very hard too.

## Light the Gospel candle

When Jesus was on earth there was once when people called him King.
It was during Jesus' hardest time.

*Welcome the Gospel. Sing Alleluia. (See page 106)*

*All stand*        *(adapted from Luke 23:35-43)*

## Gospel

Jesus was on the cross.
Above him was a sign.
"Jesus is King of the Jews."
The soldiers laughed at him.

By Jesus' side were two other men.
They were thieves.
One of them didn't care he joined in with the soldiers.
He didn't think Jesus was much of a King.

The other one did care.
He said to Jesus
"You are a good man you haven't done anything wrong.
We have done many wrong things, please don't forget me."

Jesus said,
  "I will not forget you we shall be in heaven together."

This is the Gospel of the Lord.

**Praise be to you Lord Jesus Christ.**

*All sit*

## Let's chat *(some suggestions)*

Did Jesus fight back?
What happened to Jesus after he died?

Hard times can turn into great times.
*(Leaders: explain and help the children to understand how this might be true.)*

# Some Special Feasts

Corpus Christi

SS Peter and Paul

The Transfiguration

The Assumption

All Saints

All Souls

# Corpus Christi

## Welcome

## Let's sing and say (If celebrating the Introductory Rite 2, turn to page 105)

*Quietly by yourselves*

## Stop to think

Do you eat bread every day?
Think about all the different ways you eat bread (sandwiches, burgers, pizza, toast...).

*When each child has had time to think*

## Share with one another

How many ways do you eat bread and which is your favourite?
Sometimes we don't think about the bread in our food?
We are maybe more interested in the food that we are eating it with.
Bread is important food, without it we wouldn't have pizza, etc.
Bread is both ordinary food and special food, it also makes food special.

Jesus was a person just like us, ordinary and special.
He also made our lives special.
He came from heaven.

Today we celebrate bread from heaven.
Jesus is living bread, he makes our lives special.

## Light the gospel candle

Welcome the Gospel. Sing Alleluia. (See page 106)

*All stand*          *(adapted from John 6:51)*

### Gospel

 Jesus said "I am the living bread."

This is the Gospel of the Lord.
**Praise be to you Lord Jesus Christ.**

*All sit*

## Let's chat *(some suggestions)*

It's a **bit of a riddle**.
Jesus means that he is with us everyday
(if we choose).
He is with us to help us through the ups and
downs of everyday.
We can be with him anytime of the day or
night in our thoughts.
We can also be with him in communion.

*Catechists: Remind the children.*
*Remember we don't go to communion because*
*we are good.*
*We go because we want to become good.*
*The company of Jesus will help us.*

# SS Peter and Paul

## Welcome

## Let's sing and say
*(If celebrating the Introductory Rite 2, turn to page 105)*

*Quietly by yourselves*
## Stop to think

What do you know about Peter?
What do you know about Paul?

*When each child has had time to think*
## Share with one another

*Gather as many ideas about Peter and Paul as you can.*

Peter was one of Jesus' special friends. In fact he was the leader.
Before he met Jesus he was a fisherman, a very good fisherman.
Do you remember when he changed his job?
He was a good man who tried to get the right answers to Jesus' questions.
He didn't always get them right, but he did answer the most important questions right.

## Light the Gospel candle

*Welcome the Gospel. Sing Alleluia. (See page 106)*
*All stand      (adapted from Matthew 16:13-18)*

### Gospel

Jesus asked his friends.
  "Who do you say that I am?"
Peter answered, "You are God's Son."
Jesus was very happy that Peter understood
so he made Peter leader of the Church.

This is the Gospel of the Lord.

**Praise be to you Lord Jesus Christ.**

*All sit*

## Let's chat *(some suggestions)*

Do you think Peter was pleased with his answer? Why?
He was one of the first people to recognise that Jesus is God's Son.

Paul wasn't among the first to recognise that Jesus is God's Son.
In fact it took him quite a while. He didn't like the people who followed Jesus, and he did many unkind things.

Eventually he came to his senses and he did realise
that Jesus is God's Son.
From then on he was just about one of the best friends
Jesus could ever have, and yet Paul had never seen or talked to Jesus.

How can you be a friend to someone you can't see?

What sort of of help could Peter give us?

Peter please help us to ....................................................................................

What sort of help could Paul give us?

Paul please help us to ....................................................................................

Let's sing today's song again.

# The Transfiguration

## Welcome

## Let's sing and say
(If celebrating the Introductory Rite 2, turn to page 105)

*Quietly by yourselves*
## Stop to think
Have you been anywhere wonderful this holiday?
Have you ever climbed to the top of a mountain or to the top of a building, looked out and thought, wow!

*When each child has had time to think*
## Share with one another
*Share experiences of seeing great sights and saying wow. (TV or otherwise)*
*Explain to the children the phrase, 'took my breath away'.*
When you see wonderful sights we often think, isn't God amazing.
We want to keep the moment for ever so we take photographs, and stay as long as we can.

## Light the Gospel candle
Today we hear about a wonderful moment in Jesus' life that took Peter, James and John's breath away.

*Welcome the Gospel. Sing Alleluia. (See page 106)*

*All stand*      *(adapted from Mark 9:2-10)*

## Gospel

Jesus, Peter, James and John went up a mountain to pray.
While they were there they saw Jesus talking to two men.
(Elijah and Moses)
Jesus looked absolutely radiant.
He looked wonderful.

Peter said to Jesus, "This is a wonderful place let's put up tents."
Peter hadn't finished speaking when everywhere clouded over
and became dark.
Then they all heard a voice from the cloud saying
   "This is my Son
    the chosen one.
    Listen to him."

When they looked again the two men had gone
and they were alone with Jesus so they went home.

This is the Gospel of the Lord.

**Praise be to you Lord Jesus Christ.**

*All sit*

## Let's chat *(some suggestions)*

What a wonderful day.
Which was the best part?
Do you wish that you had been there? What would you have done? Said?
Should Peter, James and John have been frightened? Why?
Who spoke?
What was God telling us?

This week while you're on holiday notice the lovely world we live in and think how glorious and wonderful God is.

# The Assumption

## Welcome

## Let's sing and say
(If celebrating the Introductory Rite 2, turn to page 105)

*Quietly by yourselves*

## Stop to think
What are the most famous stories about Mary?

*When each child has had time to think*

## Share with one another
Share and re-tell the famous stories, see how many you can remember.
Which is your favourite?
What happened in between times, in between these stories?
You will have to guess.

Mary is ............................................. mum.

This is the story of how it all began.

## Light the Gospel candle

*Welcome the Gospel. Sing Alleluia.* (See page 106)

*All stand*   *(adapted from Luke 1:26-38)*

## Gospel

One day
God sent his messenger
to a town called Nazareth
to a girl called Mary
who was engaged to a man called Joseph.
The messenger said,
"Rejoice, Mary
for the Lord has blessed you
and he is with you now."

Mary didn't know what to say
and she wondered what this meant.
But the messenger said:
"Do not be afraid –
God is very pleased with you.

Listen.
You are going to have a baby,
and you will call him Jesus."

Then Mary said:
"I am the servant of God
I am glad to do
whatever he wants."

A. J. McCallen

This is the Gospel of the Lord.

**Praise be to you Lord Jesus Christ.**

*All sit*

## Let's chat *(some suggestions)*

Which do you think was the happiest moment in Mary's life?
Which do you think was the saddest moment in Mary's life?

*Let's sing:* Which hymns do you know about Our Lady? Sing one.

*Let's pray:* Quietly in your mind talk to Mary about anything you wish.

# All Saints

## Welcome

## Let's sing and say (If celebrating the Introductory Rite 2, turn to page 105)

*Quietly by yourselves*

## Stop to think

What makes you happy?
What makes you really happy, not just excited?

*When each child has had time to think*

## Share with one another

*The children may talk about getting presents etc, help them to see happiness in other things.*
What makes the happiest time at home? When no one is shouting or arguing?
When someone praises you, thanks you and is kind to you?

The saints are happy people, really happy people.
What do you think made them happy?

## Light the Gospel candle

Jesus tells us how to be happy and how to be saints.

*Welcome the Gospel. Sing Alleluia. (See page 106)*

*All stand     (adapted from Matthew 5:1-12)*

### Gospel

 One day Jesus went up a hill and lots of people came and sat down by him.
He said to them:

"Blessed are gentle people
Blessed are people who forgive others
Blessed are people who do what's right
Blessed are people who think good
     thoughts about others
Blessed are people who make peace and
     friends with each other."

This is the Gospel of the Lord.
**Praise be to you Lord Jesus Christ.**

*All sit*

## Let's chat (some suggestions)

Listen to Jesus' list again.
Which do you think makes people happiest?

*Let's make friends*: Invite the children to shake hands, link little fingers or some other sign.
Does that make you happy?

*This week*: In some countries children celebrate the feast day of the saint they were named after more than their birthdays.
Do you know when your saint's feast day is celebrated?

# All Souls

## Welcome

It is unlikely that we will ever celebrate this feast day on a Sunday. However, your parish may still want to offer the children a chance of celebrating this feast. It may help children who have suffered a bereavement.

## Prayer

Today we remember all the people who have died.

God Our Father,
we pray for everyone who has died.
They are on their way to live with you now
so we know they will be very happy.
Help them on their journey.
Give them our love, we miss them
but we look forward to the day
when we shall be with them and you in heaven.

## Let's sing and say  *(If celebrating the Introductory Rite 2, turn to page 105)*

*Quietly by yourselves*

## Stop to think

Sometimes during the cosy evenings we miss the people who have died.
Are you missing anyone?
Think about them for a moment and quickly send them a big hug or kiss in your mind.

*When each child has had time to think*

## Share with one another

Who among your family, friends neighbours has died?
Do you know what happens to people when they die?

*(Give the children time to say what they think. Then we can tell them what we believe to be true.)*

All sorts of people say daft things.
Jesus came back from the dead so he really knows what happens.
Let's hear what he has to say.

## Light the Gospel candle

*Welcome the Gospel. Sing Alleluia. (See page 106)*

*All stand*      *(adapted from John 6:37-40)*

## Gospel

Jesus said.
"God our Father sent me into this world.
He sent me to tell you
that he wants you to live with him in heaven.
I have come to show you the way.
There is room for everyone."

This is the Gospel of the Lord

**Praise be to you Lord Jesus Christ.**

*All sit*

## Let's chat  *(some suggestions)*

There's room for everyone.
There's room for you and me. We shall all be together.
Let's always listen to Jesus so that we don't lose our way.

Make a list of all the people you know who are alive.
Think how good it is to have their company.

# Creed

We believe in God the maker of all
that we can see and can't see.
We believe in Jesus, God's Son
his only son, who lived
We believe in the Holy Spirit,
who helps us to live as Jesus did.

*or*

We believe in one God,
the Father, the Almighty.
We believe in one Lord,

Jesus Christ, the only Son of God.

We believe in the Holy Spirit,
the Lord, the giver of life.

Who proceeds from the Father and the Son.

*or*

*Song*

Fa-ther I be - lieve, Fa-ther I be - lieve, Fa-ther I be - lieve, I be-lieve in you.

Father I believe (x3)
I believe in you

Jesus I believe...

Sprit I believe...

*or*

We believe that God made the whole world.

We believe that Jesus is God and man,

that he died on the cross for us,

and that through him our sins are forgiven.
We believe in the Holy Spirit who is with the Father and Son

that through our baptism we are forgiven,

and will come to everlasting life.

# *Bidding Prayers*

There are usually about four bidding prayers, each responding to the gospel.
In these petitions we ask for whatever we need as a church, a country, a world, a parish community, to live out Jesus' teaching and create a world of peace and happiness.

The suggestions below should be **adapted**. They are offered to help introduce children to the purpose and pattern of this part of the Liturgy of the Word.

Let us pray

## May God help us to be

* kind and generous

   Lord in your mercy       R. *Hear our prayer.*

* loving and thoughtful

   Lord in your mercy       R. *Hear our prayer.*

* truthful and honest

   Lord in your mercy       R. *Hear our prayer.*

* brave and humble

   Lord in your mercy       R. *Hear our prayer.*

* helpful and gentle

   Lord in your mercy       R. *Hear our prayer.*

Hail Mary, full of grace, the Lord is with thee.
Blessed art thou among women,
and blessed is the fruit of thy womb, Jesus.
Holy Mary, Mother of God, pray for us sinners
now and at the hour of our death. Amen

## Key word for week

Which word says best how we might
live as Jesus has taught us this week?

*kind*                    *loving*                    *hopeful*
           *generous*              *thoughtful*
*truthful*                *honest*                    *brave*
           *humble*                *helpful*
                *gentle*                    ...............*other*

# Prayers

## Easter

A Prayer for the Easter Season
(alternative Gloria)

Glory, glory, glory.
Glory be to God our Father.
Glory be to Jesus our Brother.
Glory be to the Holy Spirit our friend.
Glory, glory, glory.

## November
## for the Holy Souls

We pray for our relations and friends who
have died.
They are on their way to live with you now
and we know they will be very happy.
Help them on their journey.
Give them our love, we miss them
but we look forward to the day
when we shall be with them and you
in heaven.

Amen.

## Prayers for all seasons

Hail Mary, full of grace, the Lord is with thee.
Blessed art thou among women,
and blessed is the fruit of thy womb, Jesus.
Holy Mary, Mother of God, pray for us
sinners
now and at the hour of our death.
Amen.

Our Father, who art in heaven, hallowed be
thy name.
Thy kingdom come. Thy will be done on
earth as it is in heaven.
Give us this day our daily bread, and forgive
us our trespasses,
as we forgive those who trespass against us.
And lead us not into temptation, but deliver
us from evil.

Glory be to the Father and to the Son
and to the Holy Spirit.
As it was in the beginning, is now and ever
shall be
world without end.
Amen.

# List of suggested hymns

From  *A Year of Celebration** (AYOC)      *All songs are available on a CD with lead singer

and  *Celebration Hymnal for Everyone*  (CFE)

| | *AYOC | CFE |
|---|---|---|
| **ADVENT** | | |
| An Angel came from heaven | 40 | - |
| Father, I know you are good | 43 | - |
| Sing it in the valleys | 54 | 648 |
| Light the Advent candle | - | 366 |
| **CHRISTMAS** | | |
| Away in a manger | 58 | 66 |
| I spy | 64 | - |
| Little Donkey | 68 | - |
| Little Jesus sweetly sleep | 69 | 372 |
| **CHRISTMAS/EPIPHANY** | | |
| The best gift | 75 | - |
| **LENT** | | |
| Be still and know that I am God | - | 71 |
| Lord I love you (chorus) | 90 | - |
| O Lord all the world belongs to you | 71 | 567 |
| **EASTER** | | |
| Children join the celebration | 100 | - |
| Give me joy in my heart | - | 69 |
| Give thanks | 18 | - |
| **PENTECOST** | | |
| Father we adore you | 114 | 164 |
| Shine Jesus shine | - | 388 |
| Spirit of the living God | 118 | 666 |

| | *AYOC | CFE |
|---|---|---|
| **ORDINARY TIME** | | |
| All the nations of the earth | 14 | 26 |
| Father, see your children | 177 | - |
| Let there be love | 197 | 358 |
| My God loves me | 149 | 499 |
| One more step | 129 | |
| Our God reigns | - | 268 |
| When I needed a neighbour | 160 | 800 |
| **EUCHARIST** | | |
| **Welcome** | | |
| Come Lord Jesus, come | - | 128 |
| Father see your children | 177 | - |
| Pass it on | 150 | - |
| **Gospel Acclamation** | | |
| Praise to you O Christ | - | 416 |
| **Procession of the Gifts** | | |
| All that I am | - | 23 |
| Blest are you Lord | - | 90 |
| Gifts of bread and wine | - | S3 |
| We bring our gifts | 186 | - |
| **Our Father** | | |
| Caribbean | - | 584 |
| Weiner | 191 | - |

NOTES

NOTES

# NOTES

NOTES

# A NURSERY RHYME MASS FOR ALL AGES

## Arranged from traditional melodies
## by Michael Grimmitt

Nursery rhymes are timeless:
their melodies bridge the gap between young and old.

### Musical sources:

**The Kyrie** is based on the children's playground song:
*'Poor Sarah sits a weeping on a bright summer's day'*.

**The Gloria** uses words adapted by Christopher Idle for the
hymn *'Cuddesdon'* (New English Hymnal No 363) and sets them to:
*'Sing a song of sixpence'*.

**The Sanctus & Benedictus** is based on the nursery rhyme:
*'Girls and boys come out to play'*.

**The Agnus Dei** is based on the nursery rhyme:
*'Ding Dong Bell'*
and may be sung as a round.

Published by McCrimmons
Telephone: 01702-218956   Fax: 01702-216082   Email: mccrimmons@dial.pipex.com